Feeling good and getting better

'I just want to
get it available for people
who need it,
anywhere in the world'

Rene Caisse

1889-1978

CONTENTS

Any information in this book is not to be used in substitution for a physician advise. If you have a health problem, go see a physician.

Printed by: Drukkerij Wedding, Harderwijk, The Netherlands
Art direction: Bas Barnasconi
Translated from Dutch by Merel Reinink

Preface

If someone tells you about a herbal infusion that has cured thousands of people of cancer, you're not very inclined to believe the story. It's common knowledge that medical science has to this day been unable to find a cure for cancer, so why should a herbal infusion be able to? Tall tales!

That was my reaction, too, when I first heard about Flor.Essence. But I was curious. If some people may benefit from this tea, why don't we know about it? Where did the tea originate? Which types of cancer can be treated with it? Has any research been done, and what were the results? Many questions that only fuelled my scepticism.

Curiosity won and I went looking for some answers. Without any medical background to help me, I started looking into the story of this remarkable herbal infusion. A story a hundred years old that proved to be very much alive around the world. During my journalistic research, which led me to Canada, I took in many facts, newspaper articles, medical statements, letters from people who had used the infusion, research results, and information about the Ojibwa Indians, where the tea originated. The story and the people behind the product made such an impression on me, that my interest grew - as did my need to share what I had discovered with others.

The testimonials, thousands of letters from people who were using the infusion, eventually convinced me. Healthy people, people suffering from terminal cancer, as well as those suffering from rheumatism, Alzheimer's disease, fatigue, multiple sclerosis, all reported feeling better for having used the infusion. The results varied from sleeping better and an increased energy level to the (literally) spectacular cure of tumors.

I was convinced. I am still a little apprehensive to use the word 'cure' with respect to the tea. But the fact that thousands of people have been aided by this harmless infusion was incentive enough for me to put the story to paper.

In the meantime, in Moscow, research into the effects of the infusion has been completed, confirming its efficacy. Clinical research was still in progress as this book went to press.
This book merely provides an overview of all the information available about Flor.Essence to date. It enables the reader to judge for himself and make conscious and well-informed choices regarding his health. Over the past 70 years, experiences with the tea mainly related to cancer sufferers. This book however has been written with the sincere hope that the tea can improve the quality of life of both the sick and the healthy.

Paula Bakhuis
Amsterdam, September 1997

Chapter 1

A remarkable herbal infusion

A remarkable herbal infusion

1.1 What is Flor.Essence?

Flor.Essence is the brand name for a blend of eight organic raw herbs mixed according to an original recipe of the Ojibwa Indians. By a special process a tea can be extracted from these herbs. The infusion has a detoxifying effect, supports the immune system and balances the body. Since the 1920's, many thousands of people have been treated with this herbal blend, most of whom were cancer patients. Each one of them has benefited from the use of the tea. Results varied from sleeping better and an increase in appetite, to the entire disappearance of tumors in the terminal phase. For this reason the formula - at the time still known under its provisional name Essiac - became known as a natural remedy against cancer. In later experiments, Flor.Essence was shown to also be effective in the treatment of other complaints, such as diabetes, arthritic afflictions, Alzheimer's disease, and multiple sclerosis. It can promote recovery and reduce symptoms. For a long time, the many letters from those who had used the tea, and from doctors, formed the only proof of this.
Recent pharmacological research (Moscow, 1997) confirms these experiences.
The eight herbs that make up the tea are: burdock root (Arctium lappa), sheep sorrel (Rumex acetosella), slippery elm bark (Ulmus fulva), rhubarb root (Rheum palmatum), watercress (Nasturtium officinale), blessed thistle (Carduus benedictus), red clover blossom (Trifolium pratense), and kelp (Laminaria digitata).
The synergy of these eight herbs has a cleansing and beneficial effect on all internal organs. The regular use of the herbal tea can have both a preventive and healing effect and can contribute to anyone's health. The tea is non-toxic and can be used in combination with other medicine or therapy.

1.2 Detoxification as a basis for good health

The main action of the eight herb formula is detoxification. Detoxification really only signifies the internal cleansing of the body - the removal of chemicals, toxins and other elements that are foreign to the body.
Especially in an industrialized environment, detoxification of the body is essential for good health.
The process of detoxification consists of recognizing and `breaking down' the body's refuse and the subsequent removal of it via urine, stool or sweat. Detoxification can have a positive effect on, amongst others, stool, sleep, skin, joints, digestion, mood, weight control, general energy level and endurance. In other words, you don't have to be ill to get better. Both the healthy and the sick can benefit from detoxification of the body.

A healthy body cleanses itself

A well-functioning body will get rid of toxins and chemicals all by itself. The immune system can distinguish between elements that do and do not belong in the body. Substances recognized as foreign chemicals (or xenobiotics) are removed by the nearest exit. For instance, if we swallow a dime, eventually it will turn up in the toilet bowl. If we are running a fever, perspiration will serve as a means of excreting toxins, just as diarrhoea is a physical reaction aimed at flushing harmful bacteria from our bowels. Similarly, an immune system that functions properly is able to deactivate or remove (cancer-)cells that have mutated undesirably.
The functioning of this natural system of detoxification depends on:

- our genetic or inherited ability
- the extent of the environmental burden of chemicals challenging us
- the extent to which the body is protected against exposure to these chemicals.

Exposure to toxins

Many people are unaware that their body harbors all kinds of xenobiotic toxins. These could be undigested food remnants, as well as chemicals, or toxins produced by the body itself. By estimate, these toxins could add up to several pounds every year! Toxins can enter the body through food (e.g. pesticides used on foods, medicine), through inhalation (e.g. tobacco smoke, exhaust fumes, paint), through skin contact (e.g. clothing, cosmetics) or through radiation (e.g. sunlight, X-rays, radio-therapy). Factors like stress and lack of sleep can also generate the production of harmful substances, so-called `free radicals'. Usually, the presence of toxins in the body is caused by a combination of factors. When considered per toxin, there may well not be an excessive amount of any specific toxin present. But when we consider the total amount of harmful factors our bodies have to deal with, it adds up to a substantial sum.

Those organs in our body which work to purify it, like liver and kidneys, have to work very hard to get rid of these toxins. When the amount of toxins exceeds what the body can process, toxins are stored as refuse, in organs, joints and connective tissue. At some point in time, these toxins may cause health problems. An overtaxed immune system can no longer function properly.

Chemical sensitivity

The extent to which one's health is affected by the presence of toxins partly depends on personal sensitivity to chemical elements. Some people may never experience any effects, while others may suffer from headaches, fatigue or eczema.

Complaints usually only arise after prolonged exposure to toxins, after the physical tolerance to the toxin has been exceeded. Complaints then seem to develop almost overnight. The body has developed a chemical sensitivity to the toxin.

For instance, chemical pesticides, which we swallow everyday unless we eat organic foods, can trigger symptoms once a chemical sensitivity has developed. In addition to this, there is a risk of habituation: the body is

increasingly unable to recognize a toxin as such (cf. the consumption of alcohol) and therefore the toxin is no longer decomposed and removed.
A good example of chemical sensitivity is the `Sick Building Syndrome', where large amounts of chemical substances present in the walls of modern buildings cause health problems.
According to American doctor Sherry A. Rogers, chemical sensitivity lies at the basis of many health problems of our time, such as chronic fatigue, depression, headaches and even cancer. Many of these health problems are triggered by the environment, that is, by chemicals or food.

A structural approach

Rogers calls the method of discovering the underlying causes of health problems, and the subsequent recovery of the patient, `environmental medicine'. She feels medical science should concern itself more with the structural causes of illness rather than with the treatment of symptoms.
Chemical sensitivities may manifest themselves with many different symptoms. Often, these symptoms are cerebral, such as absent-mindedness, depression, dizziness, and concentration problems.
A principle of chemical sensitivity is the spreading phenomenon. Exposure to one chemical produces susceptibility to other environmental components. This explains why people can have a hypersensitive reaction to something that has never bothered them before.
Prolonged exposure to harmful substances can cause cancer. Often, there is a connection between lifestyle, dietary pattern and the type of cancer. The relationship between smoking and lung cancer is a commonly known example; the relationship between the excessive use of saccharine and cancer of the bladder is less well-known.

What you can do against toxins

It is easier and healthier to prevent complaints rather than treat them symptom by symptom. Some symptoms that indicate the presence of toxins in the body are: a white film on the tongue, dark circles underneath the eyes, white dots on the nails, contusions, dry skin and dry hair, a

strong bodily odor or oral odor, abnormal contractions of the eye muscles and a deficient memory.
There are three things you can do to prevent health complaints as a result of toxins: detoxification, protecting the body against toxins and avoiding toxins wherever possible.

Detoxification

Visiting a sauna, an enema, fasting, the use of chlorophyl, algae supplements or nettle tea, are all ways to help the body with its detoxification process. The Indians even call it `Cleansing of Body and Spirit'. The Ojibwa herbal tea that this book is about promotes a continuous and thorough detoxification process. For this reason, daily use is recommended, although the tea, if desired, could also be used as a cleansing treatment of several weeks or months.
What happens in the body when the detoxification process is started off? Rogers uses the following description:
Phase I takes place inside the cell (in the cytosol or cell fluid) and involves chemical processes (oxidation, reduction and hydrolysis) that start to render the chemical less toxic to the body. Important components in phase I are enzymes.
Phase II detoxification takes place inside the cell as well, along a chain of molecules (enzymes) called the cytochrome P-450 system. Found in the cellular membranes, the system carries out a process called conjugation. This is where chemical groups, including glutathione and other sulfur compounds, are attached to the offending chemical in order to detoxify it. The addition of these groups serves to increase its size, polarity (electric charge) and solubility so that it can be dragged out of the body and excreted.

The practice of detoxification

Rogers' description of the detoxification process remarkably matches the experiences of many cancer patients who have used the tea. They noticed that their tumor grew harder (and smoother, as often became clear during operation), after which a kind of turning point was reached, when the tumor grew softer and then smaller. In hundreds of letters from people who had used the tea, they report finding waste material in their stool after several weeks or months.

Rogers' detoxification theory might also explain why the process of detoxification can make you very tired initially, whereas after time, your energy level increases. For each molecule of (for example) pesticide that is conjugated with glutathione to be excreted in the stool, a molecule of glutathione (the conjugate) is also lost. It costs the body energy and nutrients in order to make glutathione. The bottom line is that the work of detoxification uses up energy and nutrients.

When the nutrients needed to produce glutathione are no longer available, toxins can build up and cause health problems.

Therefore, it is advisable to use a dietary supplement during detoxification, to support the detoxification process and prevent deficiencies.

Protecting the body with healthy food

To overcome chemical sensitivity removal from the initial chemical source is not enough; you must repair the biological damage. In many cases the damage continues to progress, even though there is no further exposure. The body 'gets used to' a certain chemical and learns how to adapt the chemistry to minimize symptoms. In doing so, however, the damage merely gets shifted to another target organ. Symptoms in different target organs are not perceived as related to one another. The new disease erroneously appears to have nothing to do with previous events.

For this reason it is important to keep the body as healthy as possible, so that it can concentrate on recovering from the damage. Healthy food (see chapter 4.2) and the prevention of deficiencies are essential. Firstly, because healthy food stimulates healthy intestinal flora and the digestive process, which in turn contributes to detoxification.

But it is equally essential that through the food we eat, we obtain all the nutrients necessary for the detoxification process and our health in general: vitamins, minerals, amino acids and essential fatty acids (EFA's) with

medium chain triglycerides.
The underlying cause of chemical sensitivity can be a deficiency of a certain nutrient. Chemically sensitive people often have a taurine or cysteine deficiency. But the mineral magnesium is also very important. It is essential to the operation of some 300 enzymes in the body, many of which are needed in the detoxification process. Sometimes, a magnesium supplement alone can decrease chemical sensitivity.
Zinc also is a mineral essential to the operation of certain enzymes, and is therefore very important for the detoxification process. In addition to this it is an important stimulant for the immune system. Our body can only process some 10 percent of the zinc present in our food. If alcohol is present, this percentage is even lower. The mineral selenium is part of an enzyme that destroys harmful free radicals. Amongst other qualities, it is partly responsible for the functioning of glutathione. Selenium cleanses the body and strengthens the immune system. Our nutrition however is increasingly lacking in selenium.
The antioxidants vitamin C, vitamin E, carotenes and flavonoids in vegetables and fruit are extra important because they form a powerful line of defense against the harmful action of free radicals in our body (see chapter 4.3).
But with our current pattern of nutrition - which finds our food increasingly lacking in nutritive elements while the physical need for these elements is increasing conversely - it has become progressively more difficult to obtain all necessary nutrients. Once more it is recommended to use a natural dietary supplement, so that you can be absolutely sure that you are getting all the important nutrients in the right proportion.

Avoiding toxins

To a certain extent it is possible to avoid the toxins in our direct environment. There's not much we can do about the air we breathe, except perhaps avoiding smoky areas and refraining from smoking ourselves. Toxins that we are exposed to through food can be partly avoided by using organic food (which has not been processed and has been produced without the use of pesticides). Try to also avoid exposure to xenobiotics: for instance, don't buy new carpet if you are already suffering from Sick Building Syndrome. Try to think of ALL potential factors that may cause you problems: food allergies, washing detergent, synthetic clothing, flowers or plants, solariums, cosmetics, quilts, building insulation, amalgam fillings, tap water, etc.

It is recommended you drink some 2 litres of water every day, but you should be aware of what you are involuntarily also imbibing if you choose not to drink bottled water. Alcohol and sugar also constitute an additional burden for people who have developed chemical sensitivity.

1.3 The eight herbs and their effect

All of the eight herbs in the Ojibwa Indian herb mixture are important healing herbs. The four main herbs mentioned in this chapter are: burdock root, sheep sorrel, slippery elm and Turkish rhubarb. The remaining four herbs serve to support and increase their effect. In this chapter the effect of each herb, as it has become known over time, is described separately.

Burdock root

Botanic name: *Arctium lappa, Arctium minus*

Synonyms: *great burdock, lappa root, bardane root, beggar's button, burr seed, clotbur, cocklebur, hardock, turkey burseed (English), Grosse Klette, Klettenwurzel, Dollenkrautwurzel, Kleberwurzel (German), racine de bardane (French).*

Characteristics: *Family of the Compositae. Biennial plant that can reach over 90 centimeters high. Can be found lining ditches, rivers and roads. Flowering season July-August. Can be found all over Europe, North America, and Asia.*

Plant component used: *Root (internal), sometimes leaves (external) or seeds.*

Active ingredients: *Inulin (25-45%), mucilage 5-12%, flavonoid glycocides, bitter-glycocides (a.o. arctiopicrin), lactone, beta-sitosterol, phytoestrogens, vitamin B2, coenzyme Q-10, essential oil, iron, magnesium, chromium, silicon, zinc, sodium, potassium, thiamine, polyenes, tannins, acids (a.o. phenolic acids, tannic acids, miscellaneous organic acids) fatty acids, starches.*

Qualities:
- *restores and cleanses the skin (antiseptic)*

- *purifies the blood, cleansing for tissue and organs (depurative)*
- *stimulates excretion of urine (diuretic)*
- *stimulates transpiration (diaphoretic)*
- *lowers blood sugar level (antidiabetic)*
- *stimulates production of bile (choleretic)*
- *stimulates secretion of bile (cholagogue)*
- *tonic for liver and gall-bladder*
- *soothing for kidneys, bowels and the lymphatic system*
- *detoxicant*
- *fungicide*
- *prevents inflammations (antiphlogistic)*
- *mild laxative*
- *prevents morbid growths (antineoplastic)*
- *relieves pain (anodyne)*

Application:

- *skin complaints such as acne, eczema, flaky skin, psoriasis, boils, dandruff, dermatitis, itchy skin, seborrhoea, ringworm, staphylococcus infections, carbuncles, sores, rash, impetigo, pimples, erysipelas, very dry skin, cold sores, scrofula*
- *gout, arthritis*
- *kidney complaints, local fluid retention, stones in the kidneys or the bladder, cystitis*
- *liver and gall-bladder complaints, liver failure, stones in the gall-bladder*
- *mild cases of diabetes*
- *a high level of cholesterol in the blood*
- *syphilis, gonorrhoea*
- *hair loss*
- *prolapse of the womb*
- *abscesses*
- *digestive problems*
- *headaches, hot flashes*

Side effects: *None known so far.*

Toxicity: *Non-toxic.*

Contraindication: *Not to be used during pregnancy in view of the stimulating effect on the womb.*

Remarks

Centuries ago, burdock wine was already in use as a cleansing agent, to counter constipation and problems resulting from a stagnation in energy. Viscous soluble fibre in the root accelerates bowel transit time, absorbs toxins from the intestines, restores intestinal flora, and has a soothing effect on the mucous membranes of the intestinal canal. The root is generally used as a decoction. The seeds have comparable characteristics, but are especially considered a tonic for the kidneys. In the skin, ultraviolet light transforms the polyenes in burdock into strongly bactericidal and fungicidal substances.

Inulin, the main component of burdock, is a fructo-oligo-saccharide. It provides strength for the organism and regulates the blood sugar level. In addition to this, inulin serves as a moderator for white blood cells, which play an important part in the immune system.

Burdock and cancer

As early as in the Middle Ages, German herb-expert Hildegard von Bingen used burdock as a treatment for malignant tumors.

Centuries later, this use spread to Russia, China, India, and America. From the 1930s to the 1950s, burdock was an ingredient in the alternative cancer therapy of the American (former) miner, Harry Hoxsey.

Nowadays it can no longer be found on the list of herbs that are frequently used to treat cancer, but it is recommended for many other purposes. Yet the efficiency of this herb in battling tumors has been demonstrated in various scientific studies. In an article in Chemotherapy (1970. 15: 250), G. Dombradi qualifies the chemical arctigenin, one of the components of burdock, as 'inhibitor of experimental tumor growth'. A study by K. Morita, published in Mutation Research (1984. 129:1:25), proves that burdock prevents cell mutation in cells that are exposed to chemicals that cause such mutations.

Sheep sorrel

Botanic name: *Rumex acetosella.*

Synonyms: *Sour grass, field sorrel (English), Kleiner Ampfer (German), oseille (French).*

Characteristics: *Sheep sorrel, family of the Polygonaceae, is an annual plant which can grow to about 30 centimeters height. Has narrow, sharply pointed leaves and ears of green flowers that eventually turn red. Grows on dry ground and in pastures in most parts of the world. It blooms at the end of spring.*

Plant component used: *Leaves, stems, flowers and seeds.*

Active ingredients: *Vitamin A, vitamin B complex, vitamins C, D, E, K, P, and U, calcium, chlorine, iron, magnesium, sodium, sulfur, silicon, and traces of copper, iodine, manganese, and zinc, carotenoids (8-12%), chlorophyll, organic acids.*

Qualities:
- *stimulates excretion of urine (diuretic)*
- *stimulates transpiration (sudorific)*
- *tonic for kidneys and urinary passages*
- *refreshing, lessens thirst (refrigerant)*
- *lessens gall production*
- *invigorates the heart during a fever*

- *counteracts decay*
- *strengthens the immune system*
- *strengthens cell walls*
- *helps cleanse the blood vessels*
- *stimulates growth of new tissue*
- *increases cell oxygen content*

Application:
- *cancer (anti-mutagenic)*
- *fever*
- *scrofula*
- *cardiovascular complaints*
- *HIV/aids*
- *multiple sclerosis (MS)*
- *Parkinson's disease*

Side effects: *None known so far.*

Toxicity: *Not known.*

Contra-indication: *None.*

Remarks
Sheep sorrel is mainly taken as a decoction, but it can also be consumed raw, for instance in a salad, although not to be eaten in large quantities. The seeds have a detoxifying effect. Because of the presence of oxalic acid chrystals in the fresh leaves, one should not exceed the recommended dose.

Sheep sorrel and cancer
Historical archives of folk medicine in both Europe and the US repeatedly mention sheep sorrel as an anti-cancer herb. As early as 1740, medicinal use of the herb for cancer patients was legally sanctioned. Canadian indians used bread with sheep sorrel juice as a medicinal plaster for tumors.

Rene Caisse held this herb responsible for the breakdown of tumor tissue and various chronic complaints and degenerative disorders.
Chlorophyll, the green pigment found in the leaves, contributes to the transport of oxygen to the cells. This can prevent cell damage (incurred for example through radiation or x-rays) and can kill germs.
The anti-oxidative and anti-cancer effect of the carotenoids in sheep sorrel has also been demonstrated.

Slippery elm

Botanic name: *Ulmus rubra, Ulmus fulva, Ulmus ruba.*

Synonyms: *Slippery elm, red elm, moose elm, Indian elm (English), Rot-Ulme (German), orme rouge (French).*

Characteristics: *Slippery elm is a stately tree that can grow up to 18 meters high. Family of the Ulmaceae, originating in Central and North America. The outer bark is brown in color, but the medicinal inner bark is whitish.*

Plant component used: *Inner bark.*

Active ingredients:
Mucilage (made up of polysaccharides), vitamin A, vitamin B-complex, vitamins C, K, and P, starch and sugars, calcium, magnesium, chromium, selenium, traces of iron, phosphorus, silicon, and zinc, gallic acids, galactose, 3-methyl galactose, rhamnose, galacturonic acid, carbolic acid (a.o. tannins).

Qualities:
- *soothing for the mucous membranes (demulcent and emollient)*

- *astringent*
- *nutrient*
- *stimulates excretion of urine (diuretic)*
- *expectorant*
- *soothes the digestive system*
- *protects the stomach and reduces inflammation*
- *protects the mucous membranes of digestive tract and lungs*
- *regulates intestinal flora*
- *relieves stomach aches and reduces excess gastric juice*
- *stimulates growth of new cells*
- *vitalizes, invigorates*
- *cleanses the organs, tissues, glands and nerves of accumulated mucus and waste matter*
- *lubricant for the bones and joints*
- *antibiotic and antibacterial*
- *nerve-strengthening*

Application:
- *irritation of mucous membranes, for instance in the throat, gullet, mouth, lips, stomach, intestines, urine passages, bladder, lungs (coughing, bronchitis), vagina*
- *infections and ulcers of the mucous membranes of the stomach (gastritis), intestines (colitis), appendix, gullet (oesophagitis), rectum, colitis ulcerosa, Crohn's disease*
- *digestive problems, diarrhoea, dysentery*
- *kidney stones, gravel*
- *tissue damage through burns, wounds, operations etc. (external damage also)*
- *infirmity, exhaustion*
- *articular complaints*
- *reinforcement of muscles and tissue*

Side effects: *Some people are allergic to slippery elm tree pollen.*

Toxicity: *None.*

Contraindication
Although consulting a physician is recommended, there are no complications known of the use of slippery elm during pregnancy.

Remarks
As early as in the 18th and 19th century, the inner bark of slippery elm was very popular for its great variety of applications. It was the most frequently used herb for the relief of many complaints. The first Nation's peoples of North America used it to treat the disorders mentioned above. Because of its high nutritional value, slippery elm is often used in dietary food for the infirm.
A slimy, fibrous substance naturally forms in the plant, which can also be found in its juices. For this reason, a decoction of slippery elm will also become mucilagenous in substance once it has cooled down.

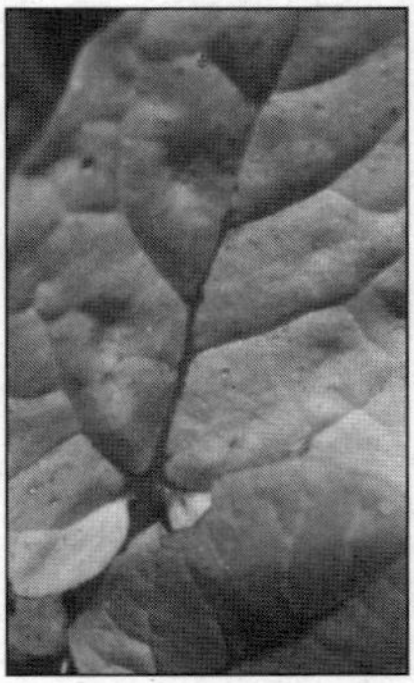

Rhubarb root

Botanic name: *Rheum palmatum, Rheum officinale*

Synonyms: *Turkish rhubarb root, Chinese rhubarb, rheum, rhubarb rhizome or root (English), Rhabarberwurzel (German), racine de rhubarbe turque (French).*

Characteristics: *Family of the Polygonaceae, found in China, Tibet, and Southern Russia. Sizeable plant which grows beside rivers high in the mountains. The roots are tuberous and richly branched. The leaves are hand-shaped (palmate) and the stem is plump and fleshy.*

Applicable plant component: *Root.*

Active ingredients: *Vitamin A, vitamin B-complex, vitamins C and P,* *calcium, chlorine, copper, iodine, iron, magnesium, manganese, phosphorus, zinc, free anthraquinones (a.o. emodin, aloë-emodin, rhein, chrysofanol, physcion), anthraquinoneglycosides (60-70%), dianthrones (making up 30-40% of the hydroxyanthracenic contents), resin, glucogallin, gallic acid, catechol, epicatechin-gallate, tannins (5-10%), bioflavonoids (a.o. rutin), polyphenols, pectin, essential oils, starch, oxalics rich in oxygen.*

Qualities:

- *mild laxative, stimulates peristalsis of the intestines*
- *stimulates excretion of mucus in the large intestin*
- *cleanses the liver*
- *stimulates excretion of gall (cholagogue)*
- *generally reinforces (tonic)*
- *strengthens the stomach (stomachic)*
- *stimulates the appetite*
- *astringent*
- *antibiotic*
- *anti-tumor*
- *against intestinal worms (anthelminthic)*
- *promotes digestion*

Application:

- *constipation, intestinal problems, inflammation of the large intestine, dysentery, bloated feeling*
- *decreased appetite*
- *liver and gall disorders*
- *hepatitis*

Side effects: *Has a constipating effect when used in small doses, but large amounts have a laxative effect. Rhubarb can render urine more yellow or even slightly red.*

Toxicity: *The leaves are toxic, which is why the fresh plant is never used.*

Contraindication (these apply to the fresh plant)
Not to be used during pregnancy (may stimulate menstruation). Also not recommended for those who suffer from gout or arthritis, kidney disorders, heartburn or acid indigestion, hemorrhoids, or while breast-feeding (renders milk bitter). In cases of intestinal obstruction (ileus) the use of rhubarb is discouraged.

Some people are allergic to rhubarb.

Remarks
There are three types of rhubarb, of which the Turkish or Chinese type is one. This herb was demonstrated to produce anti-tumor activity in the Sarcoma-37 animal test system.
Prolonged use of Rheum palmatum at high dosages can lead to a disruption of the water and electrolyte balance, and the risk of a lack of potassium. For this reason, this type of rhubarb is usually prescribed only for a short period of time. However, the amount used in the Ojibwa Indian herb mixture is so small, especially when taken in its diluted form, that even long-term use will not cause any problems.

Watercress

Botanical name: *Nasturtium officinale, Nasturtium aquatica.*

Synonyms: *Watercress, tall nasturtium (English), Echte Brunnenkresse, Brunnenkressenkraut, Wasserkresse (German), cresson, cresson de fontaine, herbe aux chantes (French).*

Characteristics: *Watercress is related to the Cruciferae and originates in*

Europe, but it can also be found in many places in North America. The plant has long, angular stems, with conspicuous, dark green leaves. Flowering season from May to September. Grows along waterways and marshes.

Applicable plant component: *Young plant (seedling).*

Active ingredients:
Isothiocyanate glycosides (glyconasturtiine in fresh plant), essential oil (rafanol), vitamins A, C, E, D and B2, carotene, minerals (a.o. iron, iodine, potassium, arsenic), bitters.

Qualities:
- *general stimulant (spleen, liver, gall-bladder, kidneys)*
- *stimulates the excretion of urine (diuretic)*
- *stimulates coughing up of phlegm (expectorant)*
- *cleanses the blood (depurative)*
- *improves blood quality*
- *improves absorption and transport of oxygen*
- *strengthens the stomach (stomachic)*
- *increases natural resistance (immunostimulant)*
- *encourages digestion (digestive)*
- *stimulant and restorative for the kidneys*
- *stimulates excretion of gall (cholagogue)*
- *lowers blood sugar level (antidiabetic)*
- *detoxificant*

Application:
- *general weakness or infirmity, fatigue, recovery from illness*
- *anaemia*
- *lung and chest disorders, cough, tightness of the chest, excess phlegm, bronchitis*
- *gout, rheumatism*
- *oedemas*
- *problematic digestion*

- *susceptibility to infections*
- *diabetes*
- *skin disorders such as rash, eczema, acne*

Side effects: *Excessive or extended use of fresh plant may cause light stomach cramps.*

Toxicity: *Not known.*

Remarks

Watercress juice is often part of a cleansing routine. It is extremely nutritious. Watercress is used in several areas of the world as a natural medicine, with various applications, including heart conditions, fever, liver and kidney complaints, gall stones, asthma, bronchitis, eczema, hepatitis, impotence and tuberculosis.

Watercress and cancer

Both Leung (1984) and Heinerman (1988) have advised carrot and watercress soup against cancer in articles. Hartwell mentions the traditional use of watercress against cancer, tumors and cysts in 'Plants used against cancer'.

Kelp

Botanical name: *Laminaria digitata*

Characteristics: *Laminaria digitata, family of the Fucaceae, is a type of seaweed. Kelp is the common name for all of these plants. Usually, these seaweeds grow on rocks below sea level. There are different varieties: Laminaria, Macrocystis and Nereocystis. The Laminaria is found on the Atlantic coast of North America.*

Plant component used: *Entire plant.*

Active ingredients: *Minerals and trace elements, especially iodine, sodium, potassium, phosphor, silicon, iron, copper, manganese, calcium, bromine, magnesium, sulfur, chlorine, and zinc. In addition to that vitamins A, C, B2, and B3, choline, vitamin E, carotene, alginates, zeaxanthin, fibre, fatty acids, saponines, carbohydrates (alginine, mannitol), mucilage.*

Qualities:
- *soothing for the digestive system (demulcent)*
- *stimulates digestion (digestive)*
- *stimulates rapid passage through intestines*
- *remineralizes*
- *regulates thyroid gland*
- *regulates the sex hormone balances*
- *promotes elimination of toxins from the intestines*
- *regulates intestinal flora*
- *protects against radiation and heavy metals*
- *protects against cardiovascular complaints*
- *promotes weight loss*
- *stimulates blood circulation, cleanses blood vessels*
- *stimulates excretion of urine (diuretic)*
- *tonic for the pituitary gland (hypophysis)*
- *induces menstruation*
- *protects against absorption of Strontium 90**

Application:
- *hypothyroidism (insufficient thyroid activity)*
- *obesity (as a result of insufficient thyroid activity)*
- *fatigue, apathy, exhaustion*
- *tuberculosis, liver and spleen disorders, syphilis (19th century)*
- *menstrual cramps*
- *ovarian cancer*

- *prostate disorders*
- *menopausal complaints*
- *enlargement of testicles or womb*
- *arthritis, rheumatism, headaches, skin disorders*
- *atherosclerosis*
- *digestive problems or constipation*
- *inflammation of the large intestine*
- *in case of radiation or when in close contact with heavy metals*
- *weak nails, hair loss*
- *involuntary contractions in the legs*
- *cellulitis*

Side effects: *May cause accelerated heartrate and speed up thyroid activity if taken in excessive dosages.*

Toxicity: *Not known.*

Contraindication (these apply to the fresh plant)
Do not use in case of high blood pressure.

Remarks

In the 19th century, kelp was commonly prescribed for its high level of iodine. Nowadays, iodine deficiencies are generally a thing of the past. The body needs 150 micrograms of iodine a day. In small doses, kelp may also prevent heart disease. Studies have indicated its ability to lower cholesterol levels and blood pressure. But kelp is also rich in sodium, which tends to heighten blood pressure. Those on a sodium restricted diet and suffering from high blood pressure should not use large amounts of kelp.

Kelp and cancer

The presence of sodium alginate in kelp helps prevent the body from absorbing radioactive Strontium 90, a by-product of nuclear explosions and weapons.

*Strontium 90 is a poisonous heavy metal, that is stored in the bones and has been associated with leukemia, bone cancer and Hodgkin's disease. Alginate supplements may reduce the level of Strontium 90 absorbtion by the body by up to 83% (The International Journal of Radiation Biology). It is only effective when used preventively.

Blessed thistle

Botanic name: *Carduus benedictus, Cnicus benedictus.*

Synonyms: *Blessed thistle, holy thistle (English), Kardobendiktenkraut, Benediktenkraut (German), herbe de chardon bénit (French).*

Characteristics: *The blessed thistle is an annual plant with grey-green, prickly leaves. It can grow up to 40 centimeters in height. The yellow flower heads are a few centimeters long. This thistle is related to the Cichoriaceae and grows in the coastal regions of the Mediterranean, South America, and South Africa. It is also cultivated for pharmaceutical purposes. Flowering season is during the entire summer. It has a bitter flavor.*

Plant component used: *All the parts above the ground.*

Active ingredients: *bitters (cnicine, benedictine), flavonoids, triterpines, phytosterols, lignans, tannins, mucilage, resin, vitamin B3, vitamin A, selenium, minerals (potassium, calcium, magnesium, chromium), essential oil.*

Qualities:
- *stimulates digestion (digestive)*
- *cleanses the blood (depurative)*
- *strengthens the nerves*

- *stimulates the metabolism*
- *antibiotic, antiviral*
- *cleanses liver and kidneys*
- *stimulates the secretion of uric acid (diuretic)*
- *stimulates the secretion of gastric juices*
- *prevents acid indigestion (heartburn)*
- *reduces flatulence (carminative)*
- *counteracts diarrhea (antidiarrheal)*
- *generally strengthening (tonic)*
- *bitter (stimulant, especially for liver and ovaries)*
- *antiseptic*
- *expectorant*
- *healing for wounds*
- *stimulant*
- *stimulates transpiration (sudorific)*
- *stimulates the appetite*
- *induces the flow of mother's milk (galactagogue)*
- *stimulates menstruation (emmenagogue)*
- *induces vomiting (emetic, only when used in high doses)*

Application:

- *fever, colds*
- *herpes, sores, boils, scabies*
- *gout, rheumatism, arthritis, backaches*
- *vertigo, deafness*
- *hepatitis, liver and gall disorders*
- *depression, amnesia*
- *headaches, migraine*
- *digestive disorders, constipation, diarrhea*
- *loss of appetite, anorexia nervosa*
- *stomach and intestinal complaints, hemorrhoids*
- *anemia, asthma, vomiting during pregnancy*
- *collection of phlegm in the lungs*

Side effects: *High doses (over 5 grams of the herb per cup of infusion) may cause vomiting and diarrhea. The therapeutic dose is safe. Some people are allergic to blessed thistle.*

Toxicity: *Not known.*

Contraindication (these apply to the fresh plant)
Not to be used during pregnancy.

Remarks
Shakespeare recommends blessed thistle in his plays for its soothing effect.

Red clover blossom

Botanic name: *Trifolium pratense, Trifolium*

Synonyms: *Rotkleebluten (German), trèfle rouge (French).*

Characteristics: *Red clover originates in Europe and Northern Africa and belongs to the plant family Leguminosae. A perennial, its flowers are ball-shaped and its leaves are arranged in triplets. Red clover is one of the oldest herbs known. It can be found along roads, in pastures, and in open country. Flowering time May-September.*

Plant component used: *Flower heads.*

Active ingredients: *Tannins, glycosides, phenols, flavonoids (pratolenin), selenium, essential oil, salicylates, caffeic acid, p-cumariczuur, calcium, chromium, magnesium, tin, thiamine (vitamin B1), niacin (vitamin B3),* *vitamin C, phosphorus, copper.*

Qualities:

- *adaptogenic*
- *phytoestrogen source with anti-estrogenic effects*
- *anti-angiogenic (stops new blood vessel formation to tumors)*
- *cleanses the blood (depurative)*
- *detoxifies (detoxificant)*
- *tonic for liver and gall bladder*
- *prevents inflammation (antiphlogistic)*
- *counteracts uncontrolled growths (antineoplastic)*
- *counteracts constipation (deobstruent)*
- *expectorant*
- *stimulates secretion of urine (diuretic)*
- *stimulates secretion of gall (cholagogue)*
- *sedative*
- *counteracts geriatric complaints (geriatric)*
- *helps build up defense mechanism against allergies*
- *possible estrogenic effect (fertility)*
- *counteracts cramps (antispasmodic)*

Application:

- *degenerative complaints caused by accumulated toxins (e.g. gout)*
- *skin complaints like acne, eczema, psoriasis, dry skin*
- *lymphatic disorders*
- *recovery from illness*
- *(whooping) cough, tightness of the chest, hoarseness, inflammation of the mammary glands*
- *auto-intoxication (self-poisoning as a result of insuffient discharge of toxins)*
- *cleansing treatment*
- *inflammation of the intestinal mucous membrane*
- *arthritis (and consequent pain)*

Side effects: *Not known.*

Toxicity: *Not known.*
Contraindication: *None.*

Remarks
Red clover is one of the main herbs used in the battle against cancer.

Red clover and cancer
Red clover has been known in various cultures for its effects on cancer for about a hundred years. In the 19th century, a group of American doctors wrote: `It unquestionably retards the growth of carcinomata.' While many present-day scientists would deny this, the anti-tumor effect of red clover has been demonstrated in several studies.
Harry Hoxsey's cancer therapy also used red clover. American doctor Jonathan Hartwell has published an article in The Journal of Natural Products in which he remarked that 33 separate cultures all over the world use red clover in the battle against cancer. Researchers of the National Cancer Institute (NCI) also found anti-tumor qualities in clover, mainly because of the presence of daidzein and genistein. In addition, red clover contains the antioxidant tocopherol, a compound of the vitamin E group. Red clover helps the body to overcome a condition called 'estrogen dominance', which is related to many forms of cancer (ovaries, breast, uterus, etc.).

1.4 Effects of the herbal tea blend

To date, the Ojibwa Indian herbal tea has not been registered as a medicine in most countries. This means that is legally covered by the Food and Drugs Act as a food without any medical claims. It is not allowed to make any connection between cases of recovery and the use of the herbal tea, since other factors may have contributed also.

In addition, each body is a unique system and may react differently. The effect of the detoxifying tea can depend on how serious the problem is, the lifestyle of the person using it, his dietary habits, any other medication or treatment he may be subject to, and of course on the patient's attitude and his determination to correctly use the tea.

There are however several standard reactions that indicate a process of detoxification and the fact that the tea is beginning to work:

- sleep may improve, since the herbal mixture has a naturally soothing effect and calms the body;
- evacuation (both through bowels and urinary passages) may improve or stabilize;
- pain may be diminished or disappear altogether;
- appetite may increase, as the taste buds may begin to work again, after having been damaged by chemotherapy or radiotherapy;
- mental attitude may become more positive and a general feeling of well-being may be experienced;
- energy level may increase;
- standard test results may show improvement.

These reactions are based on thousands of testimonials from people who have used the tea (see Chapter 6). On average, some progress can be noticed after about 3 to 6 weeks of daily use, provided the instructions for use have been followed. A short period of feebleness or nausea may be occasioned by the process of detoxification. This will occur during the initial phase, when the toxins have not yet been removed from the body. These symptoms will disappear with continued use of the tea.

The past seventy years of experience have shown, in addition to what has been mentioned above, that the herb formula:

- is a strong stimulant for the immune system;
- reduces the harmful side effects of chemotherapy and radiotherapy;
- prevents heavy metals, pesticides and other chemical substances from poisoning the body;
- removes toxin buildup, especially around the joints;
- counteracts knots and swelling and has a counterinflammatory effect.

Scientific results

Preclinical and toxicological research conducted by the Research Institute of Traditional Methods of Treatment, Health Ministery of the Russian Federation, Moscow (see Appendix IV), in 1997, has lead to the following conclusions:

Tea made with the dried herb formula Flor.Essence:

- has an stimulating effect on the immune system, especially on the immunity of the cell;
- reinforces functional activity of macrophages and neutrophiles;
- improves physical endurance and work capacity and promotes recovery of the organism after exhausting efforts;
- improves the organism's resistance against various adverse factors;
- has antitoxic, stomach and liver-protecting and antihypoxic qualities;
- protects the capillaries and precludes the development of acute inflammations caused by chemicals;
- maintains homeostasis by increasing natriuresis without changing the excretion of potassium ions;
- stimulates animal behavior, judging by parameters of spontaneous locomotory activity;
- does not effect changes in electrocardiographical parameters and arterial pressure for any of the variety of doses used in the study;
- does not cause any signs of poisoning in mice, when applied in doses equalling one, five, and ten times the maximal therapeutic dose.

1.5 Directions for preparation and use

What you need

- One packet of herbs for 1 litre herbal tea blend. If you wish to prepare 2 or 3 packets, double or triple the amount of water used.
- A covered pot (not aluminum) large enough to allow the herbal tea blend to boil vigorously without overflowing.
- A spatula or wooden spoon.
- A fine plastic or stainless steel flour strainer.
- A clean, small-mouthed glass jar (not plastic) that can be sealed. Minimal content 1 litre, brown glass is to prefer.
- Five eight ounce cups (1,25 litre) of fresh, cold (or distilled) water. Do not use fluoridated water.

Directions part I

(20 minutes)

- Measure 1,25 litre of fresh, cold (or distilled) water. Do not use fluoridated water. Place in pot, cover and bring to a boil.
- When boiling, remove pot from heat. Gently add the content of 1 packet of Dry Herbal Tea Blend into the boiling water. Stir well and cover.
- Return pot to heat. Boil for 10-12 minutes (rolling boil) covered.
- Remove pot from heat. Scrape any herbs from inside cover and sides of pot with a spatula and put them back in the liquid.
- Cover again and let stand at room temperature for 10-12 hours.

Directions part II
(30 minutes)

- When properly steeped, stir well, cover and heat tea solution to scalding (just before boiling).

- Remove pot from heat. Let settle for 20 minutes.

- Strain the liquid through a fine plastic or stainless steel flour strainer by scooping out this clear liquid with a ladle or cup, leaving the sediment in the original pot. Some sediment is OK, but try to retain mostly liquid. Do not filter. Transfer strained hot tea solution into clean, sterilized, small-mouthed glass jar(s) and close them.

- Jars must be refrigerated (do not freeze) and must be kept refrigerated at all times. Discard any opened, un-refrigerated jars. If you have prepared the tea according to the instructions above, it can be kept in the fridge for a minimum of 3 weeks. Normally, you should have finished the tea by then.

Helpful hints

- Considering the time needed for preparation, it is usually a good idea to start making the tea at night and finish making it in the morning, or vice versa.
- You may strain the tea, or scoop it out of the pot, leaving the herbs on the bottom of the pot. In that case, you will have a little less tea left over.
- Before putting the tea in the glass jar, fill the jar with boiling water, to sterilize and preheat it. Fill it with tea promptly after discarding this water.
- If your net result of liquid is less than one litre, we suggest using a deeper pot to minimize loss of water due to evaporation during the boiling stage.
- You may experience some variations in the thickness of the herbal tea blend from one batch to the next. This is due to 'mucilage', a gelatinous substance found in many plants. For those who experience difficulty in taking the tea when it is more mucilagenous, we recommend you dilute the daily amount with additional boiled water.
- The tea may be mixed with other beverages as desired, provided these beverages don't contain sugar.
- Flor.Essence is also available in liquid form. This may be a convenient solution if you're travelling, during a holiday, during hospitalization, or if you are unable to prepare the tea yourself. These bottles also need to be refrigerated after opening.

Note:

Some difference in consistency from batch to batch should not be of concern. You should know that Flora (the company that produces Flor.Essence) gets its herbs from different sources, and every harvest varies in terms of amounts of plant constituents, due to soil and climate conditions, etc.

Application

Flor.Essence may be used by anyone, with the exception of pregnant or nursing women. The daily dosis needs to be adapted for children's use. Even pets like dogs and cats may use the tea, provided the dose is adapted to their body weight (see chapter 5).

Use of the tea is especially recommended for those suffering from the following complaints:

- cancer
- multiple sclerosis (MS)
- Parkinson's disease
- arthritis, rheumatism, gout, etc.
- chronic fatigue (ME)
- tumors
- pancreas disorders
- hemorrhoids
- disorders of the prostate or urinary passages
- allergies
- psoriasis
- impotence
- warts
- asthma
- Alzheimer's disease
- sleep disorders
- diabetes

Dr. Charles A. Brusch, an American physician who researched the herb mixture for decades and treated patients with it in his own clinic, claimed that daily use of the tea 'can improve anyone's health, no matter what the problem is.'

Dosage

Flor.Essence should be taken on an empty stomach, preferably before going to bed. Taking the tea before going to sleep will lead to the best results, since the immune system builds up overnight and the tea supports that process. If you take the tea in the morning, wait at least one hour before having breakfast. The tea is best absorbed if taken on an empty stomach.

As a preventive measure

Adults who take the tea as a preventive measure should benefit from a dose of two tablespoons a day (30 ml). In some cases, this dose may be taken only every other day. If you take the tea as a preventive measure, it is not a problem if you don't use the tea for a week or so every so often, for instance by taking a week's 'rest' after each bag.

In case of illness

In case of illness or health problems, take 2 tablespoons (30 ml) of tea twice daily (morning and evening).
In almost all cases, a maximum dose of 60 ml twice daily will be sufficient. In exceptional cases, sometimes a dose of 60 ml taken 3 times a day is prescribed, but this is only the case if:
- a serious illness is involved;
- a twice daily dose of 60 ml doesn't cause any problems, but doesn't seem to have enough effect;
- the patient is very heavily built, i.e. is taller than 6 feet and weighs over 70 kilos.

When improvement has stabilized, you can go back to taking the tea twice a day. Children may also be given a preventive dose of 2 tablespoons (30 ml), but give them half in the morning and the other half in the evening, on an empty stomach. Toddlers should not be given more than 1/2 a tablespoon (15 ml) a day, half of which should be given in the morning and the other half in the evening, again on an empty stomach.
Warning: always keep the bags of dry herb mixture out of children's reach.

Helpful hint

Don't start with the maximum dose at once, but increase it gradually. If you do not suffer adverse effects from the amount you are taking, you may increase your daily dose, until you have reached the desired amount. Drink the tea slowly and take small sips; take 3 or 4 minutes to finish your cup.

Chapter 2

Rene Caisse fights for her ideal

Rene Caisse fights for her ideal

2.1 Introduction

The remarkable story of the herbal tea takes place in Canada. Canadian nurse Rene Caisse first encounters the tea in 1922 and she dedicates her long life entirely to the difficult battle for recognition of the product. Over a period of 50 years, Rene Caisse treated thousands of terminal cancer patients with tea made from the herbal mixture. Despite the many spectacular recoveries that took place in her clinic, for all the world to see, it has taken 70 years for the herbal mixture to truly become known. Nurse Caisse never asked for any compensation, nor did she accept any of the millions of dollars that were offered to her. Repeatedly, however, she was faced with the selfish and impure motives of the people who approached her with proposals to market the tea. Resolutely, almost stubbornly, she refused to release the eight-herb formula. If she was correct in acting so, it is up to the reader to decide. How could it be that Rene, shortly before she died, weary and disappointed, passed on part of the

formula to an unreliable business partner? How is it that Rene's ideal, to make the herbal tea available to everyone, didn't come true until several years after her death?
In order to be able to answer these questions, it is necessary to consider several facts more closely. For this reason, in this chapter, the main storyline is treated separately from background information. More information about the main characters can be found in the appendices.

Important information!
In this book, the term herbal mixture and Flor.Essence are used to denote Rene Caisse's original eight-herb formula, originating from the Ojibwa Indians. Officially, the name Flor.Essence has only been applicable since 1992 (when Rene's eight-herb formula was marketed under that name).
The eight-herb formula was originally called Essiac (being Rene's name in reverse). Many publications and books about the subject therefore only use the name Essiac. This might, however, lead to confusion, since a different, four-herb mixture by the same name has been on the market since the 1980's. It is often, but unjustly, argued that the four-herb formula should have the same effect as the eight-herb formula Flor.Essence. The following historical summary will demonstrate, for the first time, why that isn't the case. To prevent misconceptions, no brand name will be used to describe Rene's tea, but only descriptons such as herb mixture, herbal formula or herb tea.

2.2 Chronological summary

1889
Rene Caisse is born in Bracebridge, Ontario (Canada) in a Roman Catholic family of eleven children. Her father is of French descent, her mother is Canadian. Since there is no money to attend medical school, Rene becomes a nurse. After her training, she works in New York, until she is offered a position in Canada.

1922

Head nurse Rene Caisse is employed at the Sister of Providence Hospital in Haileybury (Ontario, Canada), when she notices a patient with a strangely scarred breast. The patient relates that she had cancer thirty years earlier and was cured by drinking a herb tea made by an old Indian medicine man of the Ojibwa Indians. Rene asks to have the names of the herbs and receives them.

This patient was an English woman, whose husband worked as a prospector in Northern Ontario. Shortly after the couple had settled in Canada, early in 1890, the then 30-year-old woman discovered a lump in her breast. The miner's camp was located near an Ojibwa Indian settlement. The couple became friendly with an old Indian medicine man, who offered to cure her. 'I have a remedy that comes from our grandfathers. A holy drink that will purify your body and place it back in balance with the Great Spirit,' the Indian said.

But the couple did not believe the story and rejected the Indian's offer.

In the hospital in Toronto, the woman's illness was diagnosed as breast cancer. Acute amputation was advised. For lack of money (back then, medical care was not available to everyone) and because she feared the operation, the woman decided to return to the Indian, after all. He gave her a herbal mixture, which he told her to drink twice a day until her body was 'back in harmony with the Great Spirit'. The medicine man also taught her how to prepare the herbal tea. After two months of using the tea on a daily basis, the woman began to notice some improvement. A year later, she was declared cured. The cancer never returned.

When Rene met this woman, thirty years later, her breast was scarred but not cancerous. Rene was told the names of the herbs in the mixture, wrote them down and decided to keep them in case she ever developed cancer herself.

1924

Rene's aunt, Mireza Potvin, is diagnosed with terminal cancer of the stomach and liver, and has been given up by doctors.
Rene asks her aunt's physician, Dr R.O. Fisher, for permission to administer the Indian tea to her aunt. After two months of daily use of the

tea, the liver tumor becomes perceptibly softer and smaller. Her aunt recovers, is declared completely free of cancer after a year, and lives another twenty years.
In cooperation with Dr Fisher, Rene begins to treat cancer patients who have been given up by their doctors. Many patients experience considerable improvement after injections with the herbal mixture. Also, more and more doctors send their hopeless cases to Rene. The Indian herbal blend gradually acquires fame.

Rene and Dr Fisher considered they might have even better results if they injected the liquid hypodermically. The first patient to receive such an injection was a man from Lyons, New York, who had cancer of the tongue and throat. With Dr Fisher and his assistent by her side, Rene injected the herbal blend straight into the patient's tongue. The man began to shake violently. His tongue became so swollen that it had to be flattened with a spatula to enable him to breathe. After twenty minutes or so, the swelling subsided and the shaking stopped. Although this patient never received another injection, the cancer stopped growing. Rene and Dr Fisher were encouraged by this result and began to experiment on mice (inoculated with human cancer) to gain more knowledge about the effect of the herbs. During this period, the formula was provisionally christened Essiac.
After two years of research, Rene and Dr Fisher had determined which particular herbs were responsible for inhibiting cancer growth. They gradually developed a formula in which one of the herbs was injected and the others were given orally. The remaining herbs seemed to promote the carrying off of destroyed tissue and infections thrown off by the malignancy, and improve the patient's general condition. For this reason, in the early years, they treated patients by injecting the tumor-inhibiting herb sheep sorrel, and administering the other herbs as an infusion.

1925

Rene is employed as a nurse at Timmins (Ontario) and, following a request from Dr J.A. McInnis, treats a woman suffering from intestinal cancer and diabetes. The patient agrees to temporarily discontinue her intake of insulin, to prevent potential complications. Six months later, the woman has recovered from cancer and she no longer needs insulin, since her diabetes has disappeared. A year later, this result is brought to the attention of Sir Frederick Banting, MD, co-discoverer of insulin. Based on the medical evidence and X-rays, Dr Banting concludes the herbal mixture had somehow stimulated the pancreas to function normally, thereby healing the diabetes.

1926

Eight doctors send a petition to the Department of National Health and Welfare in Ottowa, requesting that Rene be allowed to administer her remedy on a wide scale. The Minister of Health, Dr J.M. Robb, tells Rene she will not be interfered with as long as she doesn't charge money for her treatments.

The eight doctors were R.N. Fisher, R.A. Blye, J.A. McInnis, E.T. Hoidge, Chas H. Hair, S. Moore, H.T. William, and J.C. Robert. In their petition, they wrote: 'We, the undersigned, believe that the treatment for cancer given by Nurse R.M. Caisse can do no harm and that it relieves pain, will reduce the enlargement of tumors, and will prolong life in hopeless cases. To the best of our knowledge, she has not been given a case to treat until everything in medical and surgical science has been tried without effect and even then she was able to show remarkably beneficial results on those cases at that late stage.' Ottawa's reaction was to send two medical doctors from the Registrar of the College of Physicians and Surgeons. They carried official papers prohibiting Rene's therapy. When they heard the nurse only treated terminal cases, and was supervised by doctors, they withdrew. Dr W.C. Arnold, of the Department of National Health and Welfare, even convinced Rene to start experimenting on mice in Christie St. Hospital in Toronto, in cooperation with Dr Norich and Dr Locheed. In this laboratory, Rene ascertained that mice inoculated with human cancer had a longer life expectancy after nine injections with the herbal formula, and that their tumors became smaller.

1932

Rene has given up her nursing job to devote her time entirely to the treatment of cancer patients. From her own home in Sherbourne Street, Toronto, she treats about thirty patients every day. Later, she will move to

Peterborough, Ontario. The first major article on the herbal formula appears, in the Toronto Star: 'Bracebridge Girl Makes Notable Discovery Against Cancer', written by Roy Greenaway. Rene's fame, and that of her herbal formula, begins to grow. Rene receives several offers to market the product. She declines them all, mainly because she doesn't want to give the recipe away, fearing that it may end up with the wrong person.

1933

In June, Rene receives a letter from the Deputy Minister of Hospitals for Ontario. He is interested in finding out more about the herbal remedy, because he has heard many good things about it. Due to the efforts of Dr A.F. Bastedo, from Bracebridge, Ontario, the mayor of Bracebridge enables Rene to open a clinic in the unoccupied British Lion Hotel in Bracebridge. From 1934 to 1942, this is Rene's Cancer Clinic, where she treats patients with the eight-herb formula.

In an elaborate article about the herbal tea in a Canadian periodical, Homemaker's Magazine (1977), the situation of the clinic is described as follows:
'Dominion Street took on an atmosphere reminiscent of the famous Shrine of Lourdes, as hopeful pilgrims sought a new lease on life. Cars were parked solidly along its shoulder. People from all walks of life waited patiently to enter the red brick building. Some were carried. Others were pushed gently up the steps, while the rest managed on their own. Occasionally, an ambulance would shriek its arrival as it double-parked. Rene would be seen coming quickly down to it to treat a stretcher case. Always with a doctor standing by, she injected scores of patients every day.'
Rene's mother also became a cancer patient: she developed an incurable and inoperable form of cancer of the liver. Rene treated her with the tea without ever telling her that she had cancer. Her mother recovered, lived for another 18 years and died at the age of 90 from a heart complaint.

1936

In the Bracebridge clinic, remarkable recoveries continue to occur on a regular basis. The fame of the Canadian nurse and her natural remedy

continues to grow, with spectacular speed. She receives letters from all over the world, sometimes address only to 'Cancer nurse, Canada'. Sometimes, Rene treats over a hundred patients per day. Some of the cancer patients treated at this time are interviewed 40 years later by Homemaker's Magazine (see 1977).
A petition signed by thousands of people requests Dr J.A. Faulkner, the provincial Minister of Health, to support Rene's work. Dr Faulkner consults Dr Frederick Banting about the matter (see 1925).

Another petition was signed by nine physicians: W.H. Oaks (Rosseau), M.S. Wittick (Burks Falls), W. Dillane (Powassan), E.J. Ellis (Bracebridge), F. Shannon (Churchill), B.L. Guyatt (Toronto), J.M. Greig (Bracebridge), R.O. Fisher (Toronto), J.A. McInnis (Timmins). They strongly urged that immediate action be taken to make the herbal tea available for all cancer sufferers. Dr Frederick Banting invited Rene to test the infusion on mice in his Banting Institute in Toronto. Although Rene realized this was an important opportunity to get the tea recognized as a medicine, she declined his offer, because she did not want to leave her patients in Bracebridge behind. A decision that many people couldn't understand, but which was typical of Rene's attitude and way of looking at things. Dr Banting replied that she could take him up on the offer any time she wanted to, if she ever changed her mind. In a 1977 interview with Homemaker's Magazine, Rene said about this matter: 'Of course I am sorry that I had to decline the offer, but I would have made the same decision today.'

1937

A petition signed by 17.000 people is offered to the government. Rene Caisse and her herbal formula are the subject of a medical and political debate that reaches up to the legislature in Ontario and makes for headlines all over the country. Some American businessmen propose to create a foundation for the commercialization of the herbal formula, but Rene declines the offer. She is worried that profit may be the only concern. Rene marries her attorney, Charles McGaughey. That same year, she begins research on terminal cancer patients in Chicago.

Chicago physician Dr C. Barbourka introduced Rene to Dr John Wolfer, head of the Cancer Research Development department at Northwestern University. Wolfer made it possible for Rene to treat thirty cancer patients, all volunteers, in various stages of terminal cancer. The research project lasted a year and a half and was supervised by five physicians. They concluded that the herbal blend lengthened patients' lives, that it broke down tumors, and that it relieved pain.

Rene's life was dominated entirely by the Indian herb tea. On the weekends, she treated her patients in Bracebridge, after that, those in Toronto, still finding time to travel to Chicago every other week. At night, she would prepare the herb formula that was used for research. Probably she had lost faith in those surrounding her and insisted on doing everything herself. It was unthinkable for her to leave her Canadian patients to focus entirely on research. Doctors, who made several proposals to her to assume the permanent treatment of cancer patients in America, didn't understand her attitude.

1938

A death at the Bracebridge Cancer Clinic generates criticism of Rene and her clinic. The pathological report however states that the patient died of an embolism in the pulmonary artery, a condition brought about by a varicose condition, which the doctors had noted before. A special commission of investigation relieves Rene of all blame in the case. Despite the negative publicity surrounding the case, interest in Rene's work, and the number of patients at the clinic, continue to rise.

A never-ending stream of doctors from Canada and the US, both supporters and sceptics, visits the Bracebridge clinic. They observe the treatments with the herb formula, talk to patients, study previous cases and sometimes leave their personal testimonials.

Dr Benjamin L. Guyatt, MD, then curator of the University of Toronto's anatomy department, was a frequent visitor. He wrote about the clinic:

'In most cases, distorted countenances became normal, and the pain reduced as treatment proceeded. The relief from pain is a notable feature, as pain in these cases is very difficult to control. On checking authentic cancer cases, it was found that hemorrhage was rapidly brought under control in many difficult cases: open lesions of lip and breast responded to treatment: cancer of the cervix, rectum and bladder have been caused to disappear: and patients with cancer of the stomach diagnosed by reputable physicians and surgeons have returned to normal activity. I do know that I have witnessed in this clinic a treatment which brings about restoration through destroying the tumor tissues and supplying that something which improves the mental outlook on life and facilitates re-establishment of physiological function.'

A debate is held in the Canadian government regarding the liberal party's proposition to allow Rene to also treat non-terminal cancer patients with her herbal tea. The proposal to legalize Rene's work is accompanied by a petition signed by 55.000 citizens.
Rene's bill is defeated by just three votes, on the grounds that to allow it would be the same as endorsing her treatment as a cure or effective remedy. But a special Ontario Cancer Commission is appointed to investigate 18 experimental ways of treating cancer, including Rene's.

Rene refused to reveal the Ojibwa Indian herb formula to the Cancer Commission, arguing: 'My formula has been shown to be effective for the last 15 years, with hundreds of cancer patients. Why should I give the formula to a commission that hasn't contributed to any of that in any way, and which I now find myself defending myself against?' Her determination and somewhat naive point of view made consideration of the liberal party's proposal more difficult. Essentially, permission was asked for a non-physician to treat cancer patients with a potion made from unknown ingredients.
The investigation of the Royal Cancer Commission in formation was complicated even further. Some doctors refused to diagnose their patients on paper as cancer sufferers, because they did not want to support Rene's work. Rene and her attorney considered this to be a conspiracy, while the doctors denied it.
During the fierce debate about this matter, Rene said: 'The fact that I can get any results at all should be accepted as a good thing. When I had success, I thought the doctors would welcome me with open arms. I didn't anticipate antagonism from the profession. I would gladly give my formula to the world without any thought of gain if I knew that it would be given to humanity in the same way. I have never asked a patient for one cent.

I treated them whether they had money or not.'

All Rene wanted was recognition that cancer patients could benefit from the remedy, based on the results she had had with it over the years. With that condition, she was willing to have research take place in her clinic. On March 24, 1938, the proposal to legalize Rene's work was defeated with a margin of only three votes by the Private Bills Committee.

In August 1938, the Royal Cancer Commission was formed. It consisted of six doctors: R.C. Wallace (Kingston), R.E. Vallin (Ottawa), E.A. Collins (Copper Cliff), W.J. Deadman (Hamilton), T.H. Callahan (Toronto), G.S. Young (Toronto), and was presided by Mr Justice J.G. Gillanders.

The Royal Cancer Commission requests anyone who practices 'unorthodox' cancer treatments to send samples of their remedy, with the recipe and any other necessary information concerning treatment. Those refusing to cooperate risk a fine and potentially a prison sentence.

In reaction to this, Rene announces to her patients that she will be closing the clinic by the end of May and that she will not reopen unless the Prime Minister requests so. An effective move, because public opinion strongly demands she be allowed to reopen. The clinic opens up again and Rene is guaranteed that she will not be arrested.

1939

A crucial year for Rene with respect to the effort to obtain official recognition for the herb formula. A small sub-commission is detached to Bracebridge to interview patients and review existent material. In early March, public hearings are held at the Royal York Hotel in Toronto. 387 of Rene's patients are present, 49 of whom are heard by the Commission.

- John Thornbury testified that in 1937, his wife had been told she probably had cancer of the stomach (this had been diagnosed by X-rays). She weighed only 72 pounds and was so weakened he had to carry her into the Bracebridge clinic. Mrs Thornbury testified herself to the Royal Commission that 'I now weigh 107 pounds and can do all of my work.' (When she died, in 1975, she was 91 years old.)

- Annie Bonar had been diagnosed by biopsy at St. Michael's as having cancer of the uterus and bowel. She testified that the cancer had spread after radium treatments until her arm had swollen to double its size, and turned black. Annie Bonar: 'I went down from 150 pounds to 90 pounds, and then entered St. Michael's to have my arm amputated, but changed my mind on the eve of the operation and went to Bracebridge instead. After four months on the herbal tea treatment my arm has returned to normal, and I have gained 60 pounds.'
- John Tynon testified that he had cancer of the bowel and rectum, which had been diagnosed by four doctors: J. McDonald (Huntsville), P. McGibbon and F. Greig (Bracebridge) and A. Ardagh (Orillia). The cancer had spread through the wall of the bladder and Tynon had been operated on twice, only to hear that there was nothing that could be done. Four years after having been treated by Rene, he had gained almost 40 pounds and was a healthy man again.

The discussion between Rene and the commission gets stranded on the same issue as all previous and future discussions. The commission clearly has a problem with approving a remedy the effect of which is unclear. But Rene and her attorney feel that years of experience and results with patients that have been treated with the formula are enough proof of its effect.
The commission also lacks confidence because of Rene's refusal to release the Indian formula. Research of the effect of the herb formula should be continued and for that reason, the commission needs the formula. 'What if the formula turned out to be only water and the effect was only psychological, or if the remedy were to contain a harmful substance? The commission would make quite a bad impression if we had approved it,' the president of the commission stated.
But Rene has a very clear argument for not releasing the formula. 'If the formula becomes known, I expect that for a short time, research will be done on its effect on animals. Subsequently it will be claimed its effect can not be established. And if that happens, the remedy will never be made available to those who need it, while right now, I CAN use it to help patients.
The commission feels Rene already occupies a privileged position, since she isn't a physician but does have permission to treat patients with her

formula. But Rene, who is fifty years old by now, would like recognition for the herb formula, so it may be available to everyone. An important reason for this is the fact that it is practically not feasible that Rene for the rest of her life would be the only one who can treat patients with the tea.

In December 1939, the Commission delivers its Interim Report to Parliament. Based on research conducted with 28 cancer patients, the Report states that in cases where diagnosis had been by biopsy there was only one recovery with the herbal tea, and two improvements. In cases diagnosed by X-ray, one recovery was attributed to the tea, as were two improvements. In clinically diagnosed cases, two recoveries were attributed to the tea, and four cases of improvement were noted. The Commission feels the diagnose of cancer has been misguided in at least three cases. Ten diagnoses have been questionable, and four have not been conclusive. Only eleven cases are accepted as being cancer patients. Out of these eleven, five cures are attributed to previous radium treatments.

Rene's reaction to the verdict was quoted as follows in a daily newspaper:
'The Commission was not prepared to give the credit of any recoveries to the herb formula, if there had been any previous treatments. While I was forced to treat those patients who had been sent to me by doctors after all conventional medical treatments had failed! I was not allowed to treat patients unless they had been officially diagnosed by their physicians, and in the majority of cases, doctors would only then send me such a diagnosis when they felt there was no medical solution left.'
Ultimately, though, she felt that the outcome was moderately positive, considering the strict circumstances. Her remedy was the only one of 18 tested treatments that had brought about recovery. Strangely enough, no report of this hearing can be found in any archive. Even Rene didn't have the complete report and she didn't know where it was.

1942

After the Royal Cancer Commission report, patients experience increasing difficulty in obtaining the written diagnosis from their physicians needed for their treatment at Rene's clinic. Although Rene is never arrested, owing to the declaration by the Minister of Health, she still fears arrest and closes the clinic. Battle-weary, and according to some, bordering on a nervous breakdown, she and her husband lead a quiet and secluded life in North Bay.

1948

Rene's husband dies and Rene returns to Bracebridge. Little is known about her activities during these years. For a period of more than ten years, she remains out of the public eye. After her husband's death, Rene takes up painting and poetry. It is probable that during that time she was still treating seriously ill patients in secret. According to letters in the archives of the provincial health department, Rene treats several patients at her own home during the 1950's, an activity supervised by the health department.

1959

At age 70, Rene starts cooperating with the well-known American physician Charles A. Brusch (see appendices), a collaboration which shall prove to be of great significance for the further development of the herbal remedy.
Ralph Daigh, vice-president and director-publisher of Fawcett Publications in New York, introduces Rene to doctors at the Brusch Medical Centre in Cambridge, Massachusetts. At that clinic, and supervised by 18 physicians, Rene starts a series of treatments on terminal cancer patients and on laboratory mice. A long-held dream finally becomes reality for Rene.

One of the patients treated was Russel McCassey, suffering from basal cell carcinoma of the right cheek, which had been proved by biopsy. After four treatments with the herbal tea, the affected area changed color from red to pale pink, and then reduced in size notably. The main cancer-affected area was observed to be disappearing. Five weeks later the lesion was completely healed. Only a small scar remained, which had been caused by the biopsy.

After three months of research, Dr Brusch and Dr Charles McClure

conclude: 'Clinically, on patients suffering from pathologically proven cancer, it reduces pain and causes a recession in the growth; patients have gained weight and shown an improvement in their general health.
This, after only three months' tests, and the proof Miss Caisse has to show of the many patients she has benefited in the past 25 years, has convinced the doctors at the Brusch Medical Center that the tea has merit in the treatment of cancer. The doctors do not say that the herbal tea is a cure, but they do say it is of benefit. It is non-toxic, and is administered both orally and by intramuscular injection.'

The laboratory mice for the research project were provided by the Memorial Sloan-Kettering Institute in New York and the research was conducted by their physician Dr Philip Merker. He urged Rene to release the herb formula. As expected, she refused. The National Cancer Institute also expressed interest in the formula, but similarly to no avail. During the project, Dr McClure send questionnaires to some of Rene's former patients. A surprising number of forms was returned, bearing witness, amongst others, to the following:

Norman Thompson	Treated 20 years earlier. No regression. Still in good health in 1959.
Clara Thornbury	Treated 22 years earlier. Aged 75 in 1959 (died at the age of 91).
D.H. Laundry	Treated 11 years earlier. Aged 78 in 1959.
Nellie McVittie	Treated 23 years earlier. Aged 65 in 1969.
Wilson Hammell	Treated 31 years earlier. Still alive in 1976.
John McNee	Treated 30 years earlier. Aged 91 in 1959.
Jack Finley	Treated 20 years earlier. Aged 60 in 1959.
Lizzie Ward	Treated 14 years earlier. Aged 60 in 1959.
Mrs J.H. Stewart	Treated 16 years earlier. Aged 76 in 1959.
Eliza Veitch	Treated 18 years earlier. Aged 76 in 1959.
Fred Walker	Treated 20 years earlier. Aged 72 in 1976.

Several of her former patients were still in correspondence with Rene in 1977.

For several years Rene and Dr Brusch experience no problems. But then the laboratories suddenly stop supplying test mice, for 'diverse reasons and

technical problems'. Also, the American Medical Association prohibits her members from prescribing unknown remedies (such as Rene's tea). As a direct result, the number of patients treated with the tea is reduced dramatically.
Rene returns to Bracebridge and Dr Brusch continues working with the herbal formula, both treating patients and conducting laboratory research. He refines the formula and tests it on patients with diabetes and conditions due to high levels of toxicity.

1973

Rene (now aged 85) decides to make one more attempt. She writes a letter to the Memorial Sloan-Kettering Cancer Center in New York and is granted permission by its vice-president, Dr Chester Stock, to begin several tests with the Indian tea on laboratory mice. During the next three years, Rene sends material to the institute, to be injected in mice.

1974

Sloan-Kettering tests the herb formula on mice from the summer of 1974 up until the fall of 1976, when Rene stops sending material to the institute because the formula isn't tested according to her instructions. In 1975 Sloan-Kettering reports to Rene that some tumor-inhibiting effects have been observed in mice.

Rene always assumed human cancer cells were used, but the mice had had animal cancer cells implanted. Also, she didn't believe Sloan-Kettering was preparing the herb formula correctly. 'Last time they froze it. They might as well have been injecting distilled water!' she claimed in a 1977 interview. In her opinion, testing the formula on animal cancer was pointless. It had to be tested on patients, or, if need be, on human cancer cells implanted in animals.

1976

Rene suspects Sloan-Kettering's test methods and the results. She now refuses to supply the formula any longer, and terminates her agreement with Dr Stock.

Journalists from Homemakers Magazine visited Dr Stock, who explained that mice that have human cancer cells implanted have to go through such severe radiation treatment that this makes any reseach results unreliable at the best of times.
Notably, the material Rene had been sending to Dr Stock was 25 years old, and she only sent him the one herb that could be injected. Rene had never supplied the Sloan-Kettering Center with the complete herb formula.
Dr Stock was willing to continue testing the formula if Rene would supply him with the complete herbal mixture, with all its ingredients, so that he could combine the injections with oral administration of the tea made from the other herbs. Rene stubbornly refused.

1977

Canadian periodical Homemakers Magazine publishes extensive articles on the herbal tea in its June, July and August issues. The articles are based on several interviews reporter Sheila Snow Fraser has held with Rene, and on the work of research reporter Carroll Allen, who dug up hundreds of facts about the herb formula and tested their validity.
The article has an incredible effect and Rene finds herself at the centre of attention. A TV-documentary follows, and all the major newspapers cover the story. As a result, many patients also find their way to Rene's house and post themselves outside of it, begging to be treated with her herbal remedy.

The article in Homemakers Magazine begins as follows: 'Essentially, Rene's story was true. She had been getting remarkable results against many kinds of cancer with the herbal tea, and she had been prevented from carrying on treatment unless she revealed the formula. Whether it would have been swept under the rug by a jealous medical hierarchy, as she feared, or hailed by a grateful profession that heaped honors at her door, is a question that no one can answer, since the tea never stood the test of controlled clinical studies.'

The Homemakes Magazine journalists want to help Rene apply for a patent to the recipe and establish a foundation, so the herb formula can finally become widely available. Rene doesn't accept their proposals.

The foundation was to represent Rene in all her agreements with the government, the Cancer Institute, or any interested pharmaceutical company. The purpose of the foundation would be to speed up the process of guiding the herbal tea through the bureaucratic maze inhibiting its availability to all.

The journalists drew up the following conditions, in collaboration with Rene: the herb formula was to remain under Rene's supervision and control as long as she lived, and afterward would be controlled by the foundation; the foundation would make a concerted effort to acquire a patent for the product; a written, complete recipe for the composition of the herbal formula would be deposited in a safe, which could only be opened by Rene or someone authorized by her, and a member of the foundation's board of governors; the foundation would be dedicated to achieving research into and recognition of the Indian herb formula, supervised by Rene; the foundation would negotiate contracts which would benefit Rene Caisse.

Ultimately, Rene didn't accept any of these proposals. The journalists tried to point out to her that in the past, she had foregone many opportunities because of her incredible distrust. They drew her attention to the fact that sooner or later she would have to put her trust in someone, or the herbal blend would be doomed never to reach the people she was so anxious to help.

Rene indicated she would reveal the recipe in her testament. She didn't tell the journalists about her collaboration with Dr Brusch.

An interviewer asked her in 1977 whether she thought she had taken the right decision. Rene answered: 'I have provided help for so many people, I worked from nine to nine, often nights on end. When I saw my patients' appreciation in their eyes, when they were no longer in pain, could live a normal life again, I would think: yes. The fact that I cured my mother of liver cancer compensated for a lot of those frustrating experiences. But if I could do it all over again, I would hope for an organization to take over my work.'

David Fingard, vice-president of Canadian pharmaceutical firm Resperin, makes Rene several offers to make the formula available to Resperin, so that Resperin can market the product. Rene refuses at first, but Fingard is insistent. He says Resperin is backed by a large Canadian mining company, Dennison Mines, and therefore would have the necessary capital to make the tea widely available to 'suffering humanity'. He offers to open five

cancer clinics in Canada for the treatment of terminal cancer patients with the herb formula. The patients would only be charged a nominal fee. The proposal interests Rene. She confers with Dr Brusch and finally signs a contract with Resperin on October 26, 1977.
The events that took place during this meeting are vital with respect to the further development of the story.
Rene distrusts the Resperin proposal and makes an individual decision not to release the complete formula. This is evidenced by tape recordings made by Rene and by correspondence between Rene and radio reporter Elaine Alexander (see 1984).

The following happened: Fingard, representing Resperin, proposed to pay Rene 250 dollars each week during six months of tests with the herb formula. This amount should serve to pay for the herbs and prepare the herb formula for Resperin. If the research led to positive results, the formula would be marketed and Rene would receive two percent of the profit. Brusch considered this an abnormally small amount of money, and therefore signed the contract as a witness only. But she wasn't interested in the money. Her only aim had always been to make the herbal tea available to those who needed it. Fingard had convinced her that Resperin could guarantee this.
Rene went out of the room to retreive the formula. While she was absent, Fingard asked Dr Brusch for a financial contribution. 'Charlie,' he said, 'we need you to sign a cheque to get things off the ground.' When Rene returned and heard about this, she was furious and she didn't trust the situation. But she whispered to Dr Brusch: 'I've taken care of the situation.' She handed an envelope to Fingard, containing the names of only four of the eight herbs. Naturally, Fingard was very pleased, knowing that no one had ever succeeded before in obtaining the formula from Rene. Resperin registered the four-herb formula by the name Essiac (which until that time had been the name used by Rene and Dr Brusch for their eight-herb formula), and marketed it under that name. 'Essiac is one of the greatest discoveries in modern science,' Fingard announced to the press.

(Note: Resperin's four-herb formula from this point onwards will be denoted as Essiac, which should not be confused with the eight-herb formula, registered in 1992 under the brand name Flor.Essence.)

1978

Resperin wants to market Essiac as a registered treatment for cancer. The company begins a research project, collaborating with the Health Protection Branch of the Department of Health and Welfare to gain recognition. But like Rene, Resperin experiences problems in working with medical agencies and the project has little or no success.

The two hospitals working with Essiac use the formula in conjunction with other medicines and treatments, thereby making the research results unacceptable to the Health Protection Branch.
Several private doctors who conduct research with Essiac do not stick to the stringent guidelines imposed by the Department concerning the testing of Essiac. The cancer clinics Resperin promised to build never materialize and neither do positive research results. Rene is very disappointed.

On December 26, 1978, Rene Caisse dies aged 90, after complications following an operation on a broken hip a week earlier. She is buried close to Bracebridge. Her dream of general availability of the herb formula to all those who need it, hasn't come true.

1981

The Health Protection Branch issues an internal memo announcing that it will take steps against Resperin.

Resperin has sent Essiac to about 160 physicians to research its safety, dosage and effectiveness. Despite repeated urging by the Health Protection Branch, after several months only a few incomplete reports of inadequately performed clinical research have been received. No results can be based on this.

1982

The Department of Health and Welfare terminates the clinical testing program for Essiac, denouncing Resperin's 'flawed and worthless' research methods. It turns out Resperin doesn't have the financial platform Rene

and Dr Brusch had been promised. Resperin's failures put not only Essiac but also the eight-herb formula in a bad light. After all, no one knows that Essiac and the original formula are two different things.
Patients treated with Essiac as part of the research project protest the decision. Curiously, they receive a letter from the Department stating that Essiac has not been proven effective against cancer and that as a result, research and availability have been terminated!
Only through a difficult bureaucratic process, based on the Emergency Drug Release Program, can any patient legally acquire Essiac from Resperin, provided he or she is in a terminal stage of cancer and has an official doctor's recommendation.

Despite this being a contractual condition, Resperin did not keep Dr Brusch informed of progress in Essiac research. Dr Brusch was angry and he worried about the future of the herbal formula. Finally, he even hired a private detective to gain information about the course of proceedings at Resperin. He learned that Resperin was in a very bad state financially, and did not even function as a pharmaceutical firm. Besides David Fingard, the sole other employee was Dr Matthew Dymond, who prepared Essiac in his own kitchen with his wife and was responsible for selling the herbal mixture. Dymond was a former Minister of Health and Welfare. Both he and Fingard were in their seventies.
It soon became clear that Resperin wasn't the solid partner-in-trade Fingard had led Rene and Dr Brusch to believe. Nevertheless, for a year-and-a-half, research was done in a very inadequate way: there was little control, doctors were not furnished with the material in time, the test material differed weekly and research results were recorded insufficiently. The mess surrounding the testing of Essiac also reflected negatively on Rene's original formula, especially with the medical authorities.

1983

Meanwhile, Dr Brusch is still successfully treating cancer patients in his clinic with Rene's eight-herb formula. Dr Brusch is still determined to continue in Rene's spirit. He leaves Resperin for what it is and begins looking for other ways to recognition, which do not involve the medical authorities.

1984

Dr Brusch is diagnosed with cancer of the bowel and starts taking the herbal tea on a daily basis. He is cured, without having taken recourse to any other therapy or medicine. During a hernia-test in 1989, no sign of cancer is found. Medical documents corroborate this result.
Canadian radio reporter and producer Elaine Alexander (see appendix II) first interviews Dr Brusch in her radio show 'Stayin' Alive'.

Elaine Alexander, from Vancouver, Canada, had been a radio reporter for 20 years. In her popular new program, 'Stayin' Alive', she tackled all kinds of topical, usually controversial, health issues. She would focus on alternative as well as on conventional medicine. Elaine Alexander was so well-informed and concerned about the subject, that she almost manifested herself as another Rene Caisse. In the first interview she held with Dr Brusch, in November 1984, he told her: 'This tea is a cure for cancer. I've seen it reverse and eliminate cancers at such a progressed state that nothing medical science currently has could have accomplished similar results. I wouldn't have believed it myself had I not seen it with my own eyes. I feel very strongly that this herbal tea blend is the single most beneficial treatment for cancer today.' The radio interview leads to an unprecedented amount of reactions.

1986

From 1984 to 1986, six additional two-hour radio broadcasts about the herb formula follow, including four further interviews with Dr Brusch. Former cancer patients who have been cured through use of the tea are interviewed in the program. The public begins to see Elaine Alexander as another Rene Caisse.

66-year-old Iona Hill, from Huntsville, Ontario, told her story in the program. She had had cancer of the bowel and stomach and had been given up by doctors after an operation and five radio-therapy sessions. At the time she weighed only 84 pounds. Then she began to use the tea. After seven days, she began to feel better. Bowel movement increased and the pain stopped. After four bottles of tea, the cancer had disappeared. There were no side effects. Seven years later she called Elaine during a broadcast to tell her story. She would still use the tea occasionally.

Ron from Calgary related on air how his then three-year-old daughter had a brain tumor (phase 2) which had metastasized into the brain tissue. The doctors were powerless and gave her a maximum life expectancy of two years. Radio-therapy and very mild chemotherapy were ineffective. Rene had personally given Ron the herbal tea. She had been 88 years old at the time. Slowly, the little girl regained the abilities she had lost. On a brain scan, five years later, the tumor had disappeared. The girl was ten years old as Ron called Elaine's program.

Cancer patients inundate Elaine with letters and phone calls, and after the broadcast there are always desperate people waiting outside the studio. People find out where Elaine lives and set up camp outside her house, waiting for advice or begging for help. Elaine tries to help patients obtain the herbal tea through the Emergency Drug Release Act, but this lengthy bureaucratic process is not an option for everyone.
The situation gets out of hand. Elaine wants to help but she doesn't know how to. She works day and night. She calls '84, '85 and '86 the hardest and roughest years of her life.

1988

Elaine proposes to Dr Brusch to no longer fight for medical recognition of the herb formula. Elaine feels that the aim, to make the formula available to everyone who needs it, will not be reached by taking that difficult route. The idea rises to sell the herbs in health food stores, simply as a non-toxic, detoxifying infusion. The results will be the same, and will speak for themselves, Elaine argues. The only condition should be that the manufacturer should not legally ascribe any healing powers to the product. Elaine quits her career in radio and enters a partnership with Dr Brusch. The latter passes on to her eight herb formulas in all, of which five come from Rene Caisse. One of those is the Ojibwa Indian formula.

1989

Dr Brusch and Elaine start looking for a suitable and dedicated manufacturer for the herb formula. The manufacturer should work with biologically grown herbs of perfect quality, without chemicals, and according to an exact method of production. He should strictly observe any legislation concerning such health products. Also, he should have the ability to market the herb formula globally.

1992

Flora Manufacturing and Distributing Ltd., in Burnaby, Canada, becomes the manufacturer and distributor of the herb formula, which is sold in health food stores under the brand name Flor.Essence. Elaine Alexander starts lecturing about Flor.Essence in stores, at shows, on radio and TV. The response is incredible. At Flora, the telephone is ringing off the hook and a special office is set up to respond to callers who use the tea. Since then, every day, dozens of people have called Flora, and their data are registered by computer. Answering calls and mail about Flor.Essence, and giving information about the herb formula, has become a full-time job.

1993

Dr Charles A. Brusch dies in November, aged 91. Journalist Richard Thomas' Essiac Report, which will appear in January 1994, has already been printed at that time. This is the first book to relate the complete story of the tea, supported by many documents and patient testimonials.

1995

Flora distributes Flor. Essence to about 55 countries all over the world. The product receives the Canadian 'Alive Award', first prize in the category 'Best Herbal Medicine'.

1996

Elaine Alexander dies in April, aged 72. Her daughter Lesley inherits the rights to Flor.Essence and continues her mother's work, cooperating closely with Flora.

1997

Scientific research of the herb mixture is conducted in Moscow. Both the dry herb formula and the liquid form of Flor.Essence is subjected to toxicological and pharmacological research (see appendix IV).

Chapter 3

The Indians and their Midewiwin

The Indians and their Midewiwin

3.1 Introduction

Sometimes, Rene Caisse's herbal infusion is referred to as 'sacred Indian potion'. Some explanation is necessary. Not just because the Indians have a definition all their own of 'sacredness', but also to gain better knowledge of the origin of the tea. It is useful to know something about North American Indians in general and the Ojibwa Indians in particular; about their culture, their way of life, their spirit, and the 'Midewiwin' - the community of medicine men where the recipe of the herbal formula originates.

3.2 The North American Plains Indians

The North American prairie stretches out over some million and a half square kilometers, divided over thirteen American states and three Canadian provinces. The Indians have lived on the prairie since prehistory. But the peak period of their culture only lasted 200 years, from about 1680 to 1890.

Europeans didn't set foot on American soil until the sixteenth century. In 1534, Frenchman Jacques Cartier sailed up the St. Lawrence river, 'until he could see land on either side,' and discovered the Indian village Stadacona. In 1608, the location would become the most important base for the New France colony: the city of Quebec. During the following centuries, the old Indian territories suffered increasing pressure from European colonists. Many Indian tribes were driven away from their hunting grounds and fields, to regions that in their turn had to be ceded by other tribes.

Today, in the US, about 275 estates are reserved for Indians; in Canada, there are about 2200. North American Indians now live on these estates, on their old hunting grounds and on reservations, but they can also be found in large cities.

Farmers and nomads

Originally, many Indian tribes farmed the land. They lived in settlements during a large part of the year. These sedentary tribes often lived in earthen wigwams, covered with branches, grass and sometimes with hide or mats. A wigwam could accomodate up to 40 members of a 'family'.
Other Indian tribes were nomadic, such as the Crow, Cree, and Blackfoot tribes, and many tribes of the Sioux group. Their place of residence depended on the opportunities for hunting and on the season. They migrated throughout Northern America and were regularly involved in conflicts with settled tribes from the Rocky Mountains, who came to the prairies to hunt.
Nomadic tribes lived in the well-known teepee: buffalo-hides tied with tendons and draped around a frame of poles. Sometimes, birch-bark or other natural materials would be used. A fire would burn in the middle of the teepee, underneath the smoke hole which could be opened and closed when needed.

Buffalo and horses

The Indians lived in close relation with nature. Especially buffalo, and later horses, played an important part in their lives. For food, clothing and protection from the elements, the plains Indians depended entirely on the buffalo. The skin from the belly would be used for water-kettles, the rest of the hides was bleached, scraped and (if necessary) tanned. Buffalo hide was made into teepees, shoes and clothing. Buffalo horns and hoofs were used for various domestic utensils, buffalo hair was turned into rope, fat became soap, bones became knives, shoulder blades were turned into hoes. The meat was eaten or dried to preserve it. Naturally, hunting buffalo was one of the most important activities for the plains Indian.
When the Spaniards first introduced horses in the region, in the sixteenth century, this radically changed Indian life. The Indians had never seen a horse before. They called horses medicine dogs, Great Dog or God Dog, because dogs were the only type of pack animal they had known up to then.

The use of horses made hunting buffalo much easier. The Indians became excellent horsemen. Horses made the Indians into hunters and warriors rather than farmers. Also, now they could catch more buffalo than they needed for their own sustenance, which led to barter trade and wealth. But there was a reverse side to this: horses could be traded for guns. As more Indians owned guns, their wars became bloodier.
The buffalo were the staple food for 50.000 plains Indians. The influence of white people contributed significantly to the slaughtering of incredible amounts of buffalo. When these animals began to disappear, the Indians began to migrate to other regions. At the end of the nineteenth century, the buffalo was virtually extinct, while historical evidence indicates that once, some 60 million buffalo roamed the prairie...

Culture is nature

For Indians, culture and nature are closely related to each other. After all, nature determined their food, their way of life, but also their art, clothing, rituals and medicine.
Indians had very particular ideas about the earth, water, heaven, animals and plants. They regarded earth, literally 'mother nature', as a real mother, someone you love very much. Long before the Europeans arrived the Indians had learned to use everything nature supplied them with. Partly because this was practical, to survive. But also because nature featured in their legends, visions and rituals.
For instance, Indians allocate a specific type of tree to each human character type. Children are taught at an early age which trees they can address and how they can reach inner harmony by practising certain tree ceremonies.
Indian belief is also expressed in their feelings of solidarity with the animal realm. Indians consider animals equal to humans, sometimes even as a superior being and therefore 'holy'. Holy in this context doesn't mean divine, but signifies a combination of mystery, power and 'the aid of the powers of nature'.
According to this belief, not humans but animals rule the hunting

grounds. An important position is held there by, amongst others, the bear, elk, beaver, pine marten, porcupine and wolverine.

Rituals and customs

The best known Indian rituals are the Sundance and the smoking of the peace pipe. But there were many more customs which are still in evidence today.

Within the Indian tribe, it was very important to gain the respect of other tribe members. Respect meant personal protection and safety. Causing danger for the tribe was heavily punished.

Not every tribe had a chief, but each tribe had its experts. There were hunting experts, domestic experts and herb experts, and their advice was closely observed. Expertise led to respect and authority. For this reason, older tribe members were treated reverentially.

But respect was also due to children. Love, respect and understanding were important when raising children, but children were certainly not spoilt. At an early age, children had to acquire resilience and self-discipline, because this would prove useful to them in times of food shortage and cold, war or sickness.

During puberty, boys and girls were separated and prepared for their role as an adult. Boys looked for their 'guardian spirit', went hunting, went out on war expeditions and learned how to ride.

Girls learned to perform typically feminine tasks like gathering food, managing the teepee, and decorating clothes.

The latter could be a very prestigious task, since some war apparel contained a complete description of acts of war and battle scenes, making them into a form of calendar. Besides stories from the oral tradition, these were often the only historical registrations.

As for food, buffalo meat was the staple food. Depending on the tribe and the region, other animals were also hunted: snakes, locusts, rats, lizards, birds, moles, rabbits, sheep, and antelopes. Non-migratory tribes occasionally ate fish. The buffalo meat diet was supplemented with various other natural products: fruit, wild rice, acorns, prickly pear, herbs, wild onions, peas and Indian cassava. In spring, they sowed sweetcorn, beans, pumpkins and sunflowers. The Indians would then leave their village to go hunting buffalo. At the end of the summer, shortly before harvesting season, they would return.

3.3 The Ojibwa Indians

In North America alone, there are over fifty Indian languages, spoken by larger and smaller groups of different tribes. Within each language, dialects have developed. The most commonly used Indian language is Algonquian, and the Ojibwa Indians also used this language. For this reason, they are often called the Algonquian Ojibwa.

The Ojibwa called themselves Anishinabe, meaning 'first man' or 'original man'. Other tribes however referred to them as Ojibwa, a name later corrupted by the French and the British into Chippewa. Other names used to denote this tribe are:

- Ojibwas, Ojibays, Otchipwe, Jibewas
- Ouchipawah, Outchibous, Ostiagahoroones
- Chipeways, Chipewyans, Chippewaians, Chippewais, Chippewyans
- Achipoes, Anishinabe
- Beaver Island Indians, Bedzaqetcha, Bungees
- Downaganhas, Pillagers, Twakanha, Wahkahtowah
- Nation du Sault, Saulteaux, Salteur, Sault Indians, Souteus

Their comparative material and spiritual wealth distinguished the Ojibwa from other tribes. They were considered one of the strongest and bravest Indian tribes. They were disciplined hunters and warriors, and were considered experts with the canoe, fishing, and trapping. They were also very socially oriented: the Ojibwa lived and worked for each other, selflessly and without exploitation.

During the winter months, when their place of residence was determined by the presence of buffalo, they lived in their teepees in small family

groups. In the summer, they would gather in larger villages.
In daily life, arts and crafts, such as finger-painting, weaving, beadwork and the decoration of clothing with shells, played an important role. A typically Ojibwa product are boxes made from birch-bark and moose hair, now available as (expensive) souvenirs. A notable characteristic of their art is the occurence of geometric figures in conjunction with floral designs, usually in primary colors, such as red, blue and black.

Ojibwa history

According to legend, during the sixteenth century, the Ojibwa, Ottawa and Potawatomi Indians came from the north of Canada as a single tribe, to settle in the upper region of Lake Huron (Ontario). There, they fell apart into three distinct tribes. They settled around Lakes Huron, Superior and Michigan, fanning out into the surrounding states of Wisconsin, Minnesota and North Dakota. It is assumed that the Indians eventually left these states again, preferring to settle north and west of Lake Superior, in the woody region of Manitoba, Ontario, and Quebec.
After 1800, about 150 years after they had first made contact with the Europeans, their social and economical culture began to change. The Ojibwa became dependent on the fur trade, which forced them to abandon many of their ancient habits. They migrated to the lower region of Lake Huron, mainly for reasons of trade. Many tribes merged with each other, and lost their individual identity.

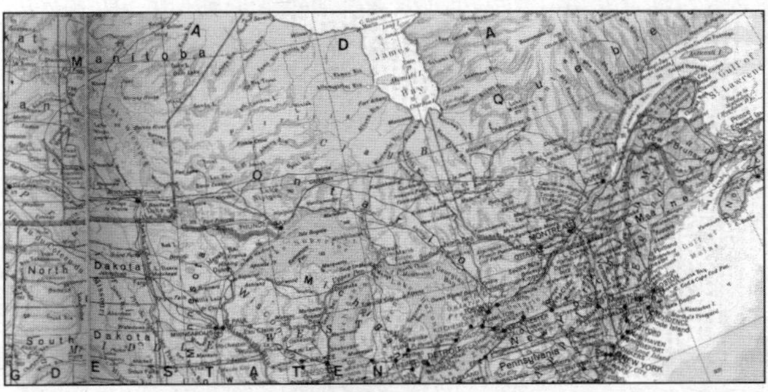

After several difficult years of war, in 1815 the Ojibwa Indians agreed to sign a treaty placing them in reservations and allotted lands in their former territories in Michigan, Wisconsin, Minnesota, and North Dakota. By estimate, around 1850, the tribe had about 28.000 members.

The Manomin

Over the centuries, the Ojibwa Indians have developed from hunters to farmers. One of the main reasons for this development is wild rice (Zizania aquatica), also called Manomin, a variety that grows without human intervention. Wild rice enabled the Ojibwa to build up food stocks, making them less dependent on food being readily available year round.

From Indian lore, an important legend about the staple food, rice:

Once upon a time, the creator of the Indians, their hero and friend Minbosho, was hungry, and he left his grandmother Nokomis to go hunting. But the old woman, who knew all the secrets of the earth, advised him to fast, for who fasts can gain knowledge of the deeper aspects of life. He went and fasted, and when his hunger grew, he heard several plants whisper: 'One day, they will eat us.' He asked the plants whom they were speaking to, and they answered: 'To you, Manibosho.' Then he dug up the root from the plant that had spoken, ate it, and got sick. Weak and hungry, he continued. Many other plants spoke to him on the way, but he dared not eat their roots.
Finally he came to a large river, in which many plants grew closely together. They, too, whispered: 'Manibosho, one day, they will eat us.' Manibosho picked several of the ripe grains, liked them and ate and ate, and this time, he did not get sick. So he asked the plants: 'What is your name?' And they answered him: 'We are called Manomin, wild rice.'
As soon as he had discovered the wild rice, he brought the news to his grandmother and told the Indians what he knew.
The rice should be honoured. It has never been planted by man, it was lain in the rivers and lakes, when the land assumed its shape for the Indians.
Nor can the rice be sown. Like the elk, the bear, the deer, the ducks, and the

partridges, like the fish and the berries, and the many other gifts from Manibosho, rice was given to us.
That's why it's holy to us.

(from: Indians of North America, Eva Lips)

The Ojibwa Indians were very well-informed about the cultivation of rice, but growing rice was also closely linked to rituals and magic. 'The Ojibwa Indians have an intimate knowledge of nature,' wrote Eva Lips, who spent a year among the Ojibwa with ethnologist Julius Lips, and studied the tribe. 'Each breath of wind is perceived and explained, the coming and going of various kinds of birds is seen in close connection with the rice growing.'

Religion and rituals

Current Ojibwa religion is a mixture of Christian beliefs and native religions. The Ojibwa believe in a Great Spirit, which is neither good nor bad. It dwells above the earth and is sometimes associated with heaven, or symbolized by the sun, or by food.

The Ojibwa believe that death affects only the body and that the human spirit (the soul) travels to another country after death. Man is completely dependent on animals and plants that have come before him. In order to survive, he has to live in close relationship with animals, plants and several spirits.

The Ojibwa religion is really all about power: energy, force, and spiritual powers. Young Ojibwa Indians for instance have to develop an 'open attitude' so that they can have a vision. Guided by an elder, the young Indian spends time in isolation, fasting, to create this open attitude. In the resulting vision, his 'guardian spirit' will reveal itself to him. Each Indian must follow his guardian spirit, and can depend on the spirit's help.

Illness, death, and accidents are considered to be caused by natural circumstances, but evil spirits and magic can also play a part. People with very strong characters, so-called shamans, can influence the powers of nature. Shamans are also responsible for all kinds of rituals, for instance the calling of spirits to cure the sick.

The Midewiwin

To gain even more 'power', the Ojibwa Indian can try to join the Midewiwin or Grand Medicine Society.

The Midewiwin is a highly sophisticated medico-religious society that preserves and passes along a vast store of plant and herbal lore for the purpose of securing good health and curing illness. The healing power of medicine men and women is based in both knowledge and the use of supernatural powers. In addition, they teach others to lead a good life. Their high moral code serves as an example to others.

To join the Midewiwin, the novice has to pass eight grades or degrees, of which the last four are the most taxing and difficult. The entire initiation period can last years, sometimes even spanning several decades. Only very few eventually pass. As a certificate of acknowledgment for grades passed, and the transfer of power, a birch bark scroll is covered with holy drawings. Most of these ancient scrolls, now on view in museums, depict visions, war exploits, songs and Midewiwin rituals. Since they were only meant for members of the Midewiwin, they could often only be interpreted by them.

The Midewiwin probably originates sometime in the 18th century. Its combination of religion and medicine was still in practice a century later in important Ojibwa settlements in Wisconsin, Minnesota, Ontario, and Manitoba. Increasing influence of Europeans and other Indian tribes led to the gradual disappearance of its rituals. Currently, only a few Ojibwa tribes still practise the Midewiwin.

3.4 Medicine wheels

Indian and Midewiwin religion and beliefs are declared in medicine wheels. These are very old holy circles or life wheels one could consider an Indian Bible. The medicine wheel is not easily described exactly. Maybe it is best compared to the significance of the cross to a Christian. It is a source of spiritual power for the Indian.
Medicine wheels have a very broad significance. They signify healing, but are also succesful in many other territories: in love, protection during a fight, or against evil. Because spirituality and medicine wheels were highly significant for the Midewiwin, the medicine wheel needs some explanation.

The structure of the wheel

A medicine wheel could be constructed by placing 36 stones on the ground. This is also an easy way of describing the elements of the wheel and, however vaguely, picturing the wheel.

The central stone is the holy altar, where the Great Spirit resides (comparable to God). In pictures, he is often symbolized by an eagle. Around the central stone are twelve smaller stones, forming a large circle. These symbolize snow goose, otter, mountain lion, hawk, beaver, deer, woodpecker, sturgeon, bear, raven, snake, and moose. In the medicine wheel, they symbolize the two-legged human being.
Around the central stone, seven additional stones symbolize the seven spiritual messagers of the Great Spirit. These are owl, mountain lion, hawk, coyote, wolf, bear, and raven.

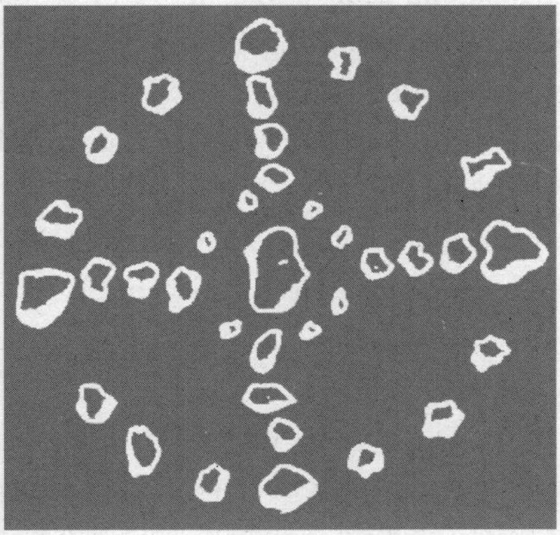

The four stones on either side of the Great Spirit indicate east, south, west, and north. They represent the four directions of the wind or powers. In medicine wheel interpretations, these four stones are sometimes seen as representing other elements, such as the four seasons, the four races, the four elements of nature, the four chakras, or the four gospels.
Finally, twelve stones are placed along the directions of the wind, forming the paths to the altar of the Great Spirit. The traditional Indian will pray to the Great Spirit every day, following the four directions.

The circle of balance and harmony

The medicine wheel could be called the wheel of life. Like life itself, it is never-ending. The altar of the Great Spirit is situated in the centre, while man is located in the outer circle. The altar is seen from a different point of view by each individual person.
All these different points of view are valuable and they add greater import to our own perspective. In other words, each individual's point of view is valued and can be of use to another person. For this reason, an Indian tribe will never try and convince another tribe that its point of view or religion is better.
The philosophy of the medicine wheel is that we do not lead a balanced life unless all the powers of the medicine wheel are used in connection. By developing your powers in one direction only, you disturb your balance. But by freely moving around the wheel, by keeping an open attitude towards other points of view, and even towards other medicine wheels, you will become a more balanced human being and will experience a more profound life.
A harmonious and balanced life should contain elements from all of the following directions (of the wind):

The east

In the east, the sun rises and the new day begins. Darkness fades before the sunlight. The color of this direction is yellow. The east is the home of the spirit of innocence, which can teach us about childhood and renewal. After all, each day is begun in innocence, as a new start, filled with faith. The spirit of resurrection also lives here, teaching us about joy, spontaneity, courage, and dedication. The east also symbolizes the spirit of enlightenment, teaching us about hope, faith, and love.

The south

In the south, the sun reaches its highest point and supplies most of its light; this direction is (usually) white in color. This is the direction that teaches us about elders, about being creative and productive, about growth and development. Because of its great warmth, the south can teach us about emotions, joy and anger, love and gratitude. It teaches us to determine a goal and show determination. We must familiarize ourselves with the (spiritual, physical or mental) powers of the south and use these for the benefit of others.

The west

In the west, the sun sets; the color of this direction is black. Black is the night, darkness, mystery. The west is home to the spirit of introspection. It is the direction of meditation, silence, thought, and being alone with ourselves.

The cleansing and healing waters come from the west. Therefore, prayers for recovery from illness are always directed towards the west. The sun setting in the west also reminds us of old age, and the knowledge gathered by the elders. The west teaches us to respect the elders and other people's convictions. It also teaches us about dreams and about dedication to others and to ourselves.

The north

This direction is red, the color of blood and life. The north houses the spirit of courage and wisdom.

Harsh winter storms hail from the north. Genuinely vital power is needed to weather the storms, whether they are physical, sociological, psychological, philosophical, spiritual, or any other kind of storm. Storms test our vigor, they strengthen us to withstand even greater difficulties, and thus lead the way to growth.

The north teaches us about the completion of the life cycle, just as all circles are completed in the north. We are taught about wisdom, understanding, insight, old age, connectivity, about the solution to problems. The north supplies traditions and ceremonies, which also generates respect for our elders and their wisdom. The spirit of the north helps us to keep a level head during our spiritual quest for the meaning of life.

Chapter 4

Supplementary measures

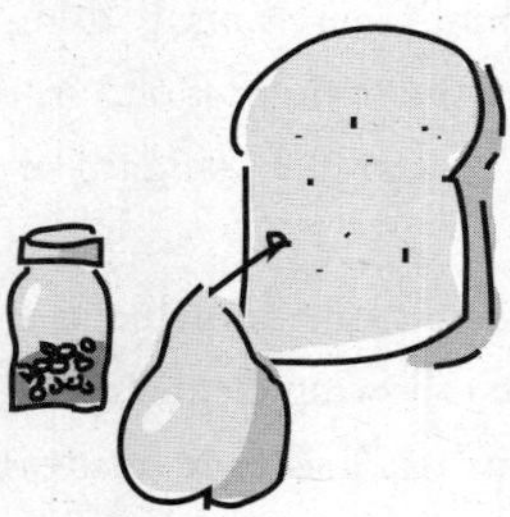

Supplementary measures

4.1 Natural medicine and phytotherapy

Being healthy involves much more than simply not being sick. That notion has been at the basis of natural medicine for centuries. Natural medicine stresses the preservation of good health and the prevention of illness. This makes natural medicine not just a form of medicine, but a way of life.
A physician practising natural medicine will not just consider the symptoms of a certain illness, but he will also look into fundamental factors like eating habits, stress and environmental pollution. Food is the basis of natural medicine.
This holistic approach to health and illness dates back to the days of Hippocrates (about 400 BC). While the contemporary idea was that illness was caused by magic or supernatural powers, Hippocrates tried to explain illness by considering natural phenomena. His followers called this approach 'vis medicatrix naturae': the healing power of nature, based on the body's ability to heal itself.

Three basic principles

One of the first definitions of natural medicine dates back to 1902, when Benedict Lust, teacher and initiator of natural medicine in the United States, published the following definition:
'The natural system for curing disease is based on a return to nature in regulating the diet, breathing, exercising, bathing and the employment of various forces to eliminate the toxic products in the system, and so raise the vitality of the patient to a proper standard of health.'

This 'natural system', as it was called, included a naturopathic cure program consisting of the following elements:

- elimination of evil habits (such as over-eating, worry, or the use of alcohol)

- corrective habits (correct exercise, improved breathing)
- initiation of new principles of living (e.g. healthy food, fasting, hydrotherapy)

During the nineteenth century, the rise in the production of synthetic medicine gradually drove natural medicine to a less prominent position. Today, natural medicine has been restored to its position as a respected science, especially since we are now aware of the side effects of synthetic medication and have begun to look for alternatives.
The three basic principles of natural medicine have remained the same through time: 'educating' patients about a healthy way of living, supporting the self-healing abilities of the body, and applying non-toxic, natural therapies. In addition, the patient's personal commitment to the healing process is vital.

Phytotherapy

The term natural medicine covers several methods of treatment or specialisms, such as homeopathy, dietetics, acupuncture, phytotherapy, iriscopy and hydrotherapy.
Phytotherapy or herbal medicine involves the treatment of complaints and illnesses solely with the aid of botanical, natural materials. (The Greek term *phyton* means plant, *therapeia* means medical treatment). In phytotherapy, the plant or its active ingredients are used to produce medication, such as extracts, tablets or capsules. Phytotherapy prefers to use either the entire plant or a specific part of it. The plant components are mutually enhancing (synergetic) or complement each other, and side effects of one element may be annihilated by another.
'Each herb contains a unique combination of chemicals. The medicinal effect results from synergetic activity of all the chemicals in the herb.' writes Dr Laurence Badgley in his book Energy Medicine.
The use of the plant in its entirety is an important difference with synthetic drugs, which merely isolate or synthetically reproduce the plant's active ingredient, thus increasing the risk of side effects. In addition, the

plant's quality determines the effectiveness of its ingredients. Method of cultivation, climate, time of harvest and processing are all factors that influence the plant's quality. Of course, natural medicine precludes the use of chemical pesticides, fertilizer and other contaminating factors such as heavy metals or radioactivity.

4.2 Healthy nutrition

Good, varied nutrition must be the single most contributing factor to good health. Healthy nutrition can help prevent illness, but it can also make a vital contribution to recovery from illness. Antioxidants (see 4.3) in vegetables and fruit for instance can help the body to counteract the influence of harmful substances and repair damaged cells.
Healthy nutrition is a prerequisite of a healthy lifestyle, which should also include:

- plenty of physical exercise or sports
- no smoking or chewing of tobacco
- a very moderate exposure to sunlight
- prevention of stress, regular relaxation
- weight control
- plenty of fresh air
- avoiding radiation and electromagnetic fields
- regular health tests (depending on age)

Nutrition and cancer

It is plausible that there is a relationship between nutrition and cancer, but the degree to which this is the case depends on many different factors. Each form of cancer has its specific causes. The relationship between nutrition and cancer of the bowels, for instance, is much stronger than that between nutrition and skin cancer. The relative importance of the role of nutrition also depends on the phase the illness is in.

Nevertheless, nutrition will always influence the patient's condition. A sick body must reserve all its energies for recovery and therefore benefits greatly from a sufficient supply of the right nutrition and energy. In addition to being healthy, food should also taste good, which is particularly important if the patient suffers from loss of appetite.
Those suffering from illness may have very different nutritional needs than healthy people. In case of illness it is very important to seek the advice of a dietician.

Guideline for healthy nutrition

Everybody seems to know what healthy food is, yet white flour, sweets, pasta, cola, margarine, instant potato puree and salad oil from the local supermarket still crowd our kitchen cabinets. A lot remains to be improved where our dietary habits are concerned. The following summary provides some elementary directions.

Eat fresh and varied food

To prevent deficiencies in important nutritional elements, it is important to have a varied diet. Try and replace bread with muesli or oatmeal sometimes, and vary between potatoes, rice, and wholewheat pasta. In the use of fruit and vegetables, too, more variation is possible. If you eat seasonal produce, it is easy to eat variedly. In addition, you may vary by eating different parts of plants: leaves (such as spinach), stalks (e.g. celery) and subterranean parts (e.g. carrots).
Inevitably, some nutritional elements are lost during processing, whether you cook, cut or freeze. For this reason, fresh produce is always preferable.

Avoid white flour

Almost all of a grain's unique nutritional elements are lost when its hull and germ are removed, as occurs during the production of white flour. So, any product made from white flour lacks these important nutritional elements. And that doesn't just apply to white bread, but also to pastas, white rice, cookies, cake, pudding and sauces created from white flour.

Replace these with healthier alternatives, like wholewheat flour, wholewheat bread, unpolished rice, and wholewheat pasta.

Avoid sugar

Chapter 1.2 already mentioned sugar as a factor that disturbs the immune system. The reason for this is partly because sugar hinders the transport of vitamin C. Most people are aware that sugar is bad for the teeth. But it can cause other problems too.

Sugar withdraws important minerals like calcium and chromium from the body, while it doesn't contribute anything other than 'empty calories'.

Sugar is a nutrient for bacteria, yeast, fungi and cancer cells. It can significantly raise the production of adrenalin, thus promoting stress. In addition, sugar can link proteins (cross-linking) and it can speed up the aging process.

There's not much point in replacing white sugars with other forms of sugar, such as honey, raw cane sugar or corn syrup, for health reasons. Because our body instantly transforms any kind of sugar into hard fats, in order to prevent the toxic effects of an excess of sugar. However, sweetening power, flavor, and influence on the blood sugar level do differ for each type of sugar.

It is important to distinguish between natural sweeteners (sometimes sorbitol and xylitol), nature-identical, man-made varieties (sorbitol, xylitol, mannitol) and synthetic sweeteners. Synthetic sweeteners are foreign to the body and their use is strongly discouraged.

Replace saturated fats by essential fatty acids (but don't use them for frying)

It is important to distinguish between good and bad types of fat. Good types of fat are essential fatty acids (EFA's), as can be found in flax oil, fish oil and wheat-germ oil. These essential fatty acids are vital for the operation of all cells, tissues, glands and organs in our body. They are rich in essential omega-3 fatty acids, prevent cancer, supply more energy, support the immune system and have an antioxidant effect in the body.

The potential danger of any diet with a reduced fat intake is that we don't

ingest enough of these good types of fat.
The way in which fats are prepared is also of influence. In a refining process, for instance, harmful trans fatty acids come into being. If good types of fat are overheated during processing, oxidation takes place, burning the oil and causing the development of dangerous peroxides. A good type of oil, rich in EFA's, can thus become very unhealthy if heated (see preparation).
Bad types of fat are animal, saturated fats, which can be found in (amongst others) pork and cheese. These types of fat are harmful if we ingest them in larger quantities than we can process. Saturated fats can promote cancer, damage the immune system and contribute to causing well-known health problems like heart and cardiovascular disease, high cholesterol levels, cancer, diabetes, multiple sclerosis, arthritis and premenstrual syndrome (PMS).
Contemporary food has a high fat content, and the ratio of saturated fats to EFA's is 10:1. It should be 1:1.

Eat high fibre foods
As a nutrient, fibre has no significance: it can't be digested. But fibre is very important to the regulation of our digestion and the functioning of the bowel. In addition, fibre contributes to a balanced blood sugar level, which is very important for diabetics and those who suffer from hypoglycemia.
Foods high in fibre are bran, wholewheat bread, and unpolished rice, but also fruit and vegetables (particularly the skins), pulses, peanuts and sweetcorn.
Fibre makes the contents of the bowel softer and more voluminous, so high fibre foods make the passage through the intestines much faster and easier, provided that you also drink sufficiently. In addition, fibre is a good source of food for the intestinal flora, which in their turn are responsible for several antibodies. In this way, fibre supports the immune system.
More and more often, a high fibre diet is linked to the prevention of cancer of the bowel.

Drink sufficient amounts of water

Drinking plenty of water is very important to our health in general and to the removal of toxins in particular. It supports kidney action and so helps the body to get rid of its toxic waste matter as quickly as possibly. A sufficient daily amount of water should be at least a litre and a half a day, but preferably two litres or more. The more water you drink, the more important it becomes that this water is clean. For this reason, bottled water should be preferred to tap water. Choose a type of bottled water that is low in mineral content, or that contains those minerals in which you are deficient.

Even when you have trouble eating, drinking remains all-important. Besides water, you might want to drink herb tea, stock, or fruit juices.

Avoid too much of anything

Too much, too greasy, too salty, too often: to maintain good health we should avoid 'too much' of anything. Moderate your intake of alcohol: it has an adverse effect on your health. Don't eat vegetables with a high nitrate content (such as lettuce, spinach, endives, and beetroot) more than twice a week, and preferably combine them with vitamin C.

Eating too much protein (meat, fish, dairy products, eggs, soy) is taxing for the body, since we do not possess a sufficient amount of proteolytic enzymes to break down large amounts of protein. In Western countries that have a relatively high consumption of dairy products, this problem is even more prominent. A non-vegetarian adult there may easily consume twice the amount of proteins he needs. This can cause toxins, intestinal gas, and an increased risk of bone decalcification.

Avoid frying and deep-frying

How we prepare our food is also very important: avoid fried, smoked or deep-fried products, especially those prepared on a grill or barbecue. When we fry or deep-fry food, in fact we are burning fats. That is unhealthy, no matter what type of oil or fat we use. When food is heated to this extent, its chemical structure alters, which hinders the operation of our bodies' cells.

Cancer and arteriosclerosis result from our body's inability to process these altered molecules. Raw, boiled or steamed products are the only healthy alternative.

Should you choose to fry your food, after all, try to use saturated fats such as real butter or olive oil that you use at a moderate temperature. Oils rich in EFA's are unstable, which means they are susceptible to light, oxygen and high temperatures. Used cold, they are healthy fats, but when heated to over 100 degrees Celsius, they become hazardous to our health.

Avoid toxins

Our food contains all kinds of matter that doesn't naturally belong in it, such as pesticide residue, hormones (meat), heavy metals (liver), and synthetic additives such as aroma's, colouring agents and preservatives. A more recent problem is the introduction of genetically engineered ingredients (such as soy), the effect of which on our health remains as yet unknown.

By choosing to use natural foods you can be certain that the food you eat contains no genetically engineered and synthetic ingredients. Natural food is certified organic food produced by organic farms, which use no artificial fertilizer or chemical pesticide. Biological meat contains no hormones or other synthetic additives. The cattle in organic farms is allocated more space and eats only biological feed, precluding the risk of diseases like BSE (bovine spongiform encephalopathy, causing mad cow's disease).

Health foods may be biological, but are not necessarily so. Health foods have simply been subjected to minimal amounts of processing. They are free of chemical or synthetical additives and have not been processed chemically or synthetically. For instance, health food has not been bleached, heated above a certain temperature, radiated, or refined, and it does not contain any artificial colourings, odors, or flavourings.

You can find natural and health food items at your health food store and also, increasingly, at your supermarket. Often a product carries a certification mark, which means it is a certified organic product.

4.3 Dietary supplements for maximum health

No single element of nutrition can cure cancer, by itself. But dietary supplements can be very valuable for maintaining good health and supporting a therapy or course of treatment. Scientific research repeatedly confirms that certain vitamins, minerals and other nutritional elements:

- can strengthen the immune system
- can protect the body against damage by free radicals
- can deactivate carcinogenic substances
- can counteract the growth of certain types of cancer
- can restore cancerous cells to normalcy
- can diminish the harmful side effects of radiotherapy and chemotherapy

Of course, the specific effect depends on the supplement itself, its form and the dose in which it is administered, and the condition of the person who uses it. In practical terms, dietary supplements can be used to prevent cancer and to slow down the disease's progress.

The value of dietary supplements

Balanced, nourishing nutrition is an essential basis for maintaining good health. But keeping a healthy and varied diet is not a practical feasibility for everyone. And it isn't always possible to get the optimum amount (which isn't the same as the minimum amount!) of all the necessary nutrients through food. Dietary supplements like multivitamin pills can help prevent potential deficiencies. In addition, such supplements can offer extra protection against harmful influences such as environmental pollution, radiation and stress. It is much easier to protect the body with healthy nutrition and dietary supplements than to try and avoid harmful influences altogether.

Dose and quality

Remember that excessive use is not recommended and that pills or capsules shouldn't serve to compensate for bad eating habits and an unhealthy

lifestyle. It is best to stick to the directions for use or follow your doctor's or dietician's advice. It is also important at what time of the day you take your supplements: if you divide your daily dosis up in two doses, take those in the morning and evening with your meal. When you take your supplements with your meal, the supplements will be more easily absorbed by your body, and that will also apply to the nutrients in the meal.
Choose dietary supplements with only natural ingredients, because these will promote their efficiency. Synthetic ingredients are not directly compatible with the body and for that reason won't be absorbed as easily. Dietary supplements shouldn't contain sugar, yeast, lactose or gluten, either.
Unfortunately, there are substantial differences in quality in the enormous amount of dietary supplements available. Have your physician, naturopath or knowledgeable shop assistant advise you concerning reliable brands.

Protection with antioxidants

It has been proven that many degenerative complaints, such as rheumatism, cardiovascular diseases, tumors and cataracts, are caused by excessive activity of free radicals in the body. Some free radicals are useful, such as those that come into being during fission (cell division) and under influence of the immune system. But there are also harmful free radicals: exceedingly aggressive little particles that the body manufactures under the influence of bad nutrition, cigarette smoke, air pollution, radiation or stress. To prevent our body being damaged by these free radicals, we have two options: avoiding these harmful influences, and protecting our body with antioxidants.
Antioxidants are essential nutrients like carotenes, vitamin A, vitamin E, selenium, cysteine and taurine. Antioxidants play an especially important part in the prevention and cure of cancer. Contrary to other nutritional elements, they protect the body in each phase of the illness.
Antioxidants - as the name reveals - counteract oxidation and so prevent the creation of free radicals. In addition, antioxidants stimulate the immune system, supporting potential other therapies that are being

applied.
American physician and scientist Dr Richard A. Passwater, antioxidant specialist, maintains that cancer has no chance of developing if the body contains ample amounts of antioxidants. As an example, Passwater mentions lung cancer: he argues that the cause of lung cancer is not smoking itself, but rather that smoking stimulates the production of harmful free radicals, giving cancer the opportunity to develop.
Vegetables and fruit for instance are rich in antioxidants, as are garlic and several herbs. To enable the antioxidants to do their work in the body, we also need vitamin B6, zinc and selenium. For antioxidants are not self-sufficient: only when other antioxidants and the other elements needed are present, may antioxidants offer protection against free radicals. Specially prepared antioxidant complexes are available as dietary supplements; they contain all these necessary elements in the right proportion.

Nutrients and cancer

The protective effect of vegetables and fruit in the prevention of cancer has been proven scientifically. Where vitamin preparations are concerned, it is less easy to draw unequivocal conclusions, because the results of different studies sometimes contradict each other. In addition, it may take many decades before sufficient scientific research has taken place to be able to state that a certain substance prevents cancer or promotes recovery from cancer.
In the summary below, only those nutrients are featured that have been scientifically proven to have an influence on cancer. In other words, there are strong indications that these nutrients may contribute to the prevention and cure of cancer.
Naturally, many other nutrients are also important to our health. Every day, 'new' nutrients are discovered that are invaluable to specific bodily functions. All the nutrients featured are (sometimes in combinations only) available as dietary supplements. The quantities mentioned are merely indications: individual needs may vary considerably.

Carotenes

is the generic name for different types of carotenes, of which beta carotene is the best known. When necessary, the body processes beta carotene to make vitamin A. It stimulates the immune system, protects against UV radiation, and diminishes the side effects of chemotherapy. Other carotenes, such as alpha carotene, lutein, lycopene, zeaxanthin, and cryptoxanthin also perform important tasks in the body. Lycopene for instance has been shown an important chemical for the prevention and cure of prostate cancer, and alpha carotene has proven many times more effective than beta carotene.
A combination of carotenes in a so-called carotene complex is a stronger antioxidant and has a stronger effect against cancer than beta carotene has by itself. Carotenes naturally occur in green vegetables, carrots, apricots, liver, onions and milk.

RDA*: - Therapeutic dose: 15-25 mg. (25,000-42,000 IU**)

* RDA = Recommended Daily Allowance: for those essential nutrients for which an RDA has been set by government committees, it is the amount of each of these essential nutrients required daily to prevent the symptoms of deficiency in a normal, healthy person.
** IU = International Units: the international agreed upon unit of measurement for vitamins A, D and E. (1000 IU = 0,6 mg)

Vitamin A

protects the body against the formation of carcinogenics, may normalize a cancer cell, stimulates the immune system, increases the recovering effect of radiotherapy and chemotherapy, regulates cell growth and development, increases communication between the cells (so preventing mutated cells from causing other cells to mutate). Vitamin A is a natural ingredient of liver, eggs and milk. Its efficacy increases when it is combined with vitamin C.

RDA: 2500-5000 IU Therapeutic dose: 10.000-25.000 IU

Vitamin C

is the only vitamin that it is hard to get too much of. A major antioxidant, it protects against the formation of chemicals that promote cancer (e.g. nitrite), may normalize cancer cells, stimulates the immune system, enhances the healing effect of radiotherapy, decreases the side effects of chemotherapy, stimulates the effect of vitamin E, and regulates the electric charge of enzymes. The most important natural sources of vitamin C are vegetables and fruit. As a dietary supplement, Ester-C is the easiest form to digest.

RDA: 30-60 mg Therapeutic dose: 1 or several grams in 2 doses

Vitamin E

is an antioxidant, protects the body against the formation of carcinogenics, may normalize a cancer cell, protects cell membranes and EFA's and cholesterol against oxidation, stimulates the immune system, enhances the healing effect of chemotherapy, radiotherapy, and several natural therapies, can break chain reactions. Its effect is substantially greater when combined with other antioxidants. Foodstuffs with a high level in vitamin E are vegetable oils, nuts, whole grains, vegetables and fish.

RDA: 7-10 IU Therapeutic dose: 100-800 IU

Selenium

is an important chemical in the prevention of cancer, a component of glutathione. Selenium acts as an antioxidant, strengthens the immune system, helps DNA repair itself, reduces the effect of carcinogenics on DNA, suppresses genetic mutations, chelates heavy metals and regulates various enzyme interactions. Selenium is extra effective when combined with vitamin E. The amount of selenium we ingest daily depends partly on the composition of the soil. However, it is a fact that present-day food is deficient in selenium and that suppletion is therefore desirable. Natural sources of selenium are unprocessed grains, wheat germ, brewer's yeast, garlic, onions, fruit and tuna.

RDA: 50-150 mcg Therapeutic dose: 100-200 mcg

Vitamin B complex
or the group of B-vitamins is in several ways instrumental to the prevention and treatment of cancer. B-vitamins are important for the formation of coenzymes, which themselves form many thousands of enzymes. Folic acid, choline and PABA deserve extra attention here.

Folic acid
is part of the group of B-vitamins and is responsible for healthy DNA. Damaged DNA causes deviant cell mutation. Folic acid is found in leaf vegetables, carrots, avocado, apricots, beans, wholewheat flour and eggs.

RDA: 200-400 mcg Therapeutic dose: 400-2000 mcg

Choline
is not a vitamin, but a chemical the body is able to manufacture out of the amino acid methionine. Some researchers maintain we produce insufficient amounts of choline to protect ourselves against cancer. In their opinion, a choline deficiency may, when combined with a deficiency in other chemicals, be able to cause cancer even without exposure to free radicals or carcinogenics.

RDA: - Therapeutic dose: 100-900 mg (as component of a multivitamin)

PABA
signifies para aminobenzoic acid and isn't properly a vitamin. PABA supports quite a few antioxidant processes and, when used externally, protects against solar radiation and old age. It protects the cell membranes against free radicals, promotes the production of folic acid in the bowels, and is instrumental to the absorbence of pantothenic acid. Brewer's yeast, unprocessed grains, wheat germ and vegetables are a natural source of PABA.

RDA: - Therapeutic dose: 50-500 mg

Zinc
is one of the components of the copper-zinc SOD (superoxide dismutase), protects proteins against oxidation, protects T-cells against oxidation, features in a substantial amount of enzyme reactions, is responsible for the appropriate functioning of the immune system, prevents and cures prostate ailments. A zinc deficiency can promote the generation of precancerous cells. Zinc, a mineral, works in synergy with vitamins C and taurine. Oysters, other shellfish, meat, egg yolk, brewer's yeast and beans are rich in zinc.

RDA: 10-15 mg. Therapeutic dose: 15-30 mg

Iron
helps the body combat free radicals as part of the iron SOD. When taken in excess, or when protected insufficiently by vitamins C and E, iron works as a pro-oxidant, but a deficiency may similarly lead to the formation of free radicals.

RDA: 10-18 mg. Therapeutic dose: 10-30 mg

Copper
is a component of the copper-zinc SOD, promotes the absorbence of iron, assists in rendering certain toxins harmless (cadmium). When used in excess or when insufficiently protected by vitamin C and cysteine it functions as a pro-oxidant.
Copper is naturally present in shellfish and crustaceans, liver, whole wheat, prunes and green vegetables.

RDA: 1,5-3,5 mg. Therapeutic dose: 2 mg

Chromium
belongs to the trace elements, protects cholesterol and cysteine against oxidation, promotes the glucose tolerant factor. Brewer's yeast, shellfish and crustaceans, and meat are rich in chromium.

RDA: - Therapeutic dose: 25-100 mcg

Manganese
is a mineral that activates enzymes to protect cells against being damaged by free radicals, is a component of the manganese SOD, stimulates the hypophysis when combined with PABA.
Natural sources of manganese are grain products, walnuts, seeds, ginger, and tea.

RDA: - Therapeutic dose: 2-5 mg

Other antioxidants
which have attracted cancer researchers' attention over the last few years have been sulphuric antioxidants like liponic acid and NAC (N-acetyl-L-cysteine), amino-acids with an antioxidant effect like cysteine, methionine, and taurine, and antioxidant enzymes such as SOD, catalase, and glutathione.
Other substances, such as cholesterol, chlorophyll, shark liver oil, garlic, and coenzyme Q-10 are also described more and more often in connection with their role as antioxidant in the prevention of cancer. Not all these substances are essential nutrients, since the body can itself produce these substances. Further research should determine their importance to our health.

Phytonutrients
are non-essential nutrients that occur in foodstuffs and herbs. Amongst them are many thousands of flavonoids: bioflavonoids (rutin, hesperidin, quercetin), proanthocyanidins (OPC) in red wine, flavans, flavones (luteolin), flavonones, flavonols (naringenin), isoflavons (genistein, daidzein, leucoanthocyanidines en catechins. In the body, these substances function, amongst others, as antioxidants and catchers of free radicals. In addition, they have an antibacterial, antiviral, anti-cancer, and antimutagenic effect, they protect the cell, and have many other important

functions. We ingest about a gram of flavonoids every day through our food, amongst others from grains, potatoes, vegetables, fruit, herbs, beer, wine, coffee and tea. Green tea (see 4.4) and genistein deserve particular interest.

Genistein

belongs to the isoflavons. Many research projects have shown that soy isoflavons regulate (amongst other things) the female hormone balance, are powerful antioxidants and may restrain cancer growth. One of the richest sources of genistein is the soy plant. Not surprisingly, in communities with a high consumption of soy products, certain types of cancer are less common.

The way isoflavons function in our body resembles that of the female hormone estrogen. An important difference is, however, that high levels of estrogen may be conducive to the occurence of certain types of hormonal cancer, while tumors may inversely be inhibited in their development when isoflavons are present.

Over 200 scientific publications have appeared about the effect of genistein on cancer. These have established, amongst other findings, that genistein inhibits the growth of cancer cells in cases of breast cancer, cancer of the bowel, lung cancer, prostate cancer, skin cancer, and leukemia. Genistein has proven a powerful antioxidant and it checks an enzyme (tyrosine protein kinase) responsible for the growth of cancer cells.

It has also been established that genistein supports the transition of cancer cells into healthy cells and that it checks the growth of new blood vessels which feed the tumor.

Shark cartilage

contains components that prevent new blood vessels from being formed. This prevents blood flow toward the tumor, thus depriving it of nutrients. The fact that sharks are very rarely affected by cancer and that their skeleton consists almost completely of cartilage, started Dr I. William Lane on his research into shark cartilage. He began several research projects and introduced a treatment method for cancer (especially tumors) with shark cartilage supplements.

Research has shown that shark cartilage may curb the growth of tumors and can cause existent tumors to become smaller. However, research into this subject is still in an experimental stage.

The most commonly used dose of shark cartilage is 1 gram per kilogram of body weight, dissolved in water (administered orally or rectally). There are no known side effects to the use of shark cartilage, but an allergic reaction to this type of protein is a possibility. The ingestion of shark cartilage is not recommended during pregnancy, after a heart attack, or after operations. For this reason, don't use shark cartilage without medical indication. And make sure it is of good quality.

Conclusion

Certain nutrients are of vital importance to our health and can contribute to the prevention and cure of diseases such as cancer. In our daily food, not all of these nutrients are present in the quantities required. Used in addition to a healthy diet, dietary supplements may help prevent potential deficiencies.

Individual health and needs may differ, but it is safe to say that a natural vitamin preparation, possibly supplemented with an antioxidant complex, can improve every adult's health.

4.4 Other herbs to use against cancer

All over the world, by estimate over 3,000 types of plants have been used to treat cancer. In many cases, the anti-tumor effect of plants and herbs has been scientifically demonstrated in laboratory studies, tests on humans and animals.
In some cases, herbal remedies from folk medicine have become predecessors of allopathic drugs. An example are the herbs Catharanthus roseus and Podophyllum peltatum. Cancer drugs Vincristin and Vinblastin were developed following a program in which these two herbs were tested.
There is a growing interest in the use of herbs, sometimes even as a supporting measure for conventional therapies like radiotherapy and chemotherapy. But generally, scientific research is required to bring about even the most modest form of acceptation. The high cost involved poses a barrier to many manufacturers of herbal products.
In this chapter, only those herbs most frequently used in connection with cancer will be mentioned. We shouldn't expect miracles of any of these herbs. But there are usually no side effects, which means there is no objection to trying them out. But make sure you are well-advised, because even herbs and natural substances may be taken in excess.

Green tea

Green tea is tea made from the tea plant Camellia sinensis, which hasn't been fermented. Preferably, green tea should be made out of leaves that have been on the plant for exactly three years, prior to being harvested.
The leaves of the tea plant contain many valuable substances, such as vitamins C and E, carotene, and minerals like fluoride, zinc, selenium and magnesium. Especially polyphenols, gallic acids, flavonoids, and catechins in green tea are known for their protective effect on the cell and their powerful antioxidant qualities. The absence of a fermentation process preserves these valuable substances.
Japanese government research has established that in areas with a high consumption of green tea, the death rate due to cancer (particularly cancer

of the stomach) is significantly lower. Laboratory research has also demonstrated significant antibacterial properties, while those bacteria considered beneficial were not affected.
Animal testing with green tea by the National Cancer Research Centre in Tokio and The American Health Foundation in New York, has established that drinking green tea offers 45% protection against lung cancer.
In 1997, green tea was catapulted back into the public eye by researchers, as is evidenced by an article in Nature about the preventive effect of polyphenols in green tea. In particular epigallocatechin gallate (EGCG) is responsible for this preventive effect. EGCG forms a compound with urokinase, an enzyme essential to tumor growth. By combining with the enzyme, EGCG inhibits the enzyme's actions and the growth of the tumor. An additional advantage of EGCG is that it is perfectly safe to use, even when taken in high dosages (Jankun, Selman, Swiercz, Skrzypczak-Jankun 1997). Incidentally, even a single cup of green tea a week is sufficient to lower the risk of lung cancer, esophageal cancer, and cancer of the stomach.

Astragalus (Astragalus membranaceus)

An important herb which supports the immune system is astragalus, which various studies have established to be effective in treating hepatitis, virus infections, cancer, and even AIDS. Astragalus has featured in Chinese herbal medicine for centuries, as a means of improving resistance against infections, due to its strong stimulating effect on the immune system. Research has established that astragalus has a positive influence on stamina, interferon production, and T-cell activity. It was also shown to expel excess liquid, to check kidney inflammation, and to stimulate the heart. The herb protects the liver from toxic substances, even from tetrachloride poisoning. Chinese researchers have discovered that astragalus enhances the effect of interleukin-2 (a substance which may also be used in chemotherapy), while it lessens toxic side effects. Research at the University of Houston has established that immune system cells which have been damaged by cancer may be restored by taking astragalus. Many types of T-cells are stimulated by this herb.

Mistletoe (Viscum album)

Not to be confused with the American mistletoe (Phoradendron flavescens). Mistletoe improves natural resistance, stimulates the thymus, and increases white blood cell activity. Acts against both benignant and malignant tumors. All these qualities make it a valuable herb for the support of any cancer therapy and as a follow-up treatment after a cancer operation.

The active ingredients of mistletoe are, amongst others, viscotoxin, bioflavonoids, phytosterols, amino acids, choline, triterpines, lignins and saponosides.

Iscador, a misletoe extract, has been used for over fifty years in the anthroposophical cancer clinic Lukas Klinik in Arlesheim, Switzerland. Anthroposophist Rudolf Steiner (1861-1925), who considered cancer a disharmony between cell division and cell growth, advised treatment with mistletoe. Mistletoe appears to be particularly effective in raising the odds of survival for patients with cervical cancer, ovarian cancer, vaginal cancer, breast cancer, cancer of the stomach or bowel, and lung cancer.

Ginseng (Panax ginseng)

The ginseng root is known as a general restorative herb that can be used in case of fatigue, listlessness, recovery after illness, and stress. Several of its qualities make it suitable as a support during cancer therapies. Ginseng has a normalizing effect on the immune system, is a tonic and stimulant for the entire organism and improves efficient use of oxygen and stamina. It protects the body from radiation, protects the liver against toxins, has a depurative effect on the blood, and prevents tumors.

The active ingredients of the ginseng root are, amongst others, triterpenoid saponins, phytosterols, polyacetylene derivates, polysaccharides, vitamin B complex, vitamin C, carotene, bioflavonoids, amino acids, enzymes and various minerals.

The Chinese government supports Chinese studies of Fu Zhen therapy, which aims to improve the cancer patient's immune system. This therapy, consisting of (amongst others) ginseng (Panax ginseng), privet (Ligustrum

lucidum), and astralagus, is applied in many Chinese hospitals. The privet is an olive-like shrub; its berries have a generally restorative and diuretic effect, and stimulate the defence mechanism.
Fu Zhen herbs have been shown to stimulate the functioning of T-cells. Both Chinese and American studies have established the effect of Fu Zhen therapy on various immune system related illnesses, including cancer, AIDS, and leukemia.

Hoxsey herbs

The American Harry M. Hoxsey (1901-1974) developed a herbal cancer therapy, which he claimed originated with his great-grandfather. During the 1950's, Hoxsey's clinic was the largest private cancer clinic in the world. Despite the fact that thousands of patients have been cured through Hoxsey's therapy, the therapy has been labeled an 'unestablished method' in the US. An independent research team called his herbal treatment more succesful and effective than radiotherapy, operations, and chemotherapy. Hoxsey supported his herbal therapy with vitamins, a special diet, and therapy that stimulated the immune system.
His blend of herbs consisted of:

- barberry root (Berberis vulgaris)
- buckthorn bark (Bumelia lydioides)
- burdock (Arctium lappa, also ingredient of Flor.Essence, see 1.3)
- dried bark of alder buckthorn (Rhamnus purshiana, also Cascara sagrada)
- red clover blossom (Trifolium pratense, ingredient of Flor. Essence, see 1.3)
- licorice root (Glycyrrhiza glabra)
- pokeweed root (Phytolacca americana)
- prickly ash (Xantoxylum clava-herculis, ingredient of Pro.Essence, a variety of Flor. Essence especially developed for the prostate)
- stillingia root (Stillingia sylvatica)
- bloodroot (Sanguinaria canadensis) for external use only

Of the ten herbs used by Hoxsey, seven have been proven active against tumors.

Chaparral (Larrea tridentata)

Chaparral leaves and stems have been used by Indians for centuries against (amongst others) cancer, arthritis, rheumatism, stomach problems, and skin infections.

The medical world became interested in chaparral when a man had been cured of a malignant melanoma after drinking chaparral tea. Consequent research demonstrated that chaparral has a significant ability to diminish the size of tumors.

One of the active ingredients of chaparral is nor-dihydroguairenic acid, which impairs a tumor's electron transport system, and so lessens the tumor's cell respiration. This therapy has been found particularly succesful in the treatment of melanoma (Biochemical Pharmacology, 19:2699, 1977).

Chaparral is a potent antioxidant and an antibiotic. It is particularly used to treat degenerative illnesses, caused by free radicals.

Wheatgrass (Triticum sativum)

Wheatgrass is a very rich source of SOD, which has a strong antioxidant effect and protects against all kinds of radiation.

Wheat sprouts form a rich source of vitamins (60 times the amount of vitamin C found in oranges, also vitamin B17, laetrile (which is assumed to be an anti-carcinogenic, minerals, enzymes, chlorophyll and abscissinic acid. The latter ingredient has been shown to lessen tumor size in animal experiments. Wheatgrass apparently nourishes the cells, provides them with oxygen and cleanses them of toxins. It is especially well-known for its cleansing effect on the bowels, and in addition to its detoxifying effect it also has a depurative effect on the blood, stimulates the excretion of urine, and stimulates the appetite. A Texas System Cancer Center study has established that wheatgrass has a strong anti-mutagenic effect, and that it also has a destructive effect on tumors. Some claim that is due to the fact that wheatgrass also contains iodine and selenium.

Wheatgrass is rich in oxygen and chlorophyll, which is responsible for the transport of oxygen in plants, similar to the role of hemoglobin in human blood circulation.

Reishi (Ganoderma lucidum)

The Japanese mushroom Reishi is described in traditional Chinese medicine as warming, invigorating, detoxifying, and prolonging life. This mushroom is a traditional remedy for liver complaints, cancer, asthma, bronchitis, high blood pressure, and as a general support for the immune system. The mushroom itself is valued as a nutrient, however, it's really the mycelium that's richest in active ingredients: polysaccharides, triterpines, and phytosterols.

Polysaccharides are known to increase RNA/DNA in bone marrow and they operate as antioxidants. Triterpines lower the cholesterol level and operate as ACE inhibitors, lowering blood pressure. Phytosterols stimulate the excretion of cholesterol. In addition to all this, Reishi contains oleic acid and cyclo-octasulphur, which have an anti-allergenic effect.

It appears that the combination of these active ingredients supports the immune system, amongst others by increasing the production of interferon, interleukin-1 and interleukin-2, by providing protection against radiation, by stimulating the manufacture of killer cells and white blood cells, and by protecting the liver. These qualities explain why Reiki has an antibacterial, antiviral, anti-allergenic and anti-mutagenic effect. The Japanese government and the Moscow Cancer Research Center have gone so far as to officially declare this mushroom a cancer remedy.

Shiitake (Lentinus edodes)

Shiitake, a type of mushroom, is very popular in macrobiotic and Japanese cuisine. In traditional Chinese medicine, shiitake is applied to complaints concerning the immune system, like cancer, allergies, infections, common cold, and flu. It has also been shown to have an effect on inflammations of the bronchial tubes and on high levels of cholesterol.

Several components of shiitake have been researched regularly and have been established to contain the following substances: eritadenine, which lowers cholesterol and lipoproteins, polysaccharides (including KS-2 which acts as a strong check on the growth of tumors), soluble lignins, and beta-glucanes. These components of the mushroom have been established to have an anti-tumor, antiviral, antimutagenic, blood pressure-reducing and cholesterol-reducing effect, and they also protect the liver and strengthen the immune system.

Maitake (Grifola frondosa)

Many thousands of tons of the Japanese mushroom maitake are exported every year. Maitake is a traditional remedy for high blood pressure, cancer, immune system disorders, and liver complaints. This mushroom contains many active ingredients, including polysaccharides (alpha and beta-glucanes). The effect of maitake as a dietary supplement in the treatment of cancer is currently under research in both the US and China.

Pau d'Arco (Tabebuia avellenedae)

Pau d'Arco is a tree found in Brazil, Argentina, and Peru. Its bark has been applied as a folk medicine for cancer, but also on ulcers, and in cases of diabetes, rheumatism, dysentery, and digestive disorders. It is mainly used as a supportive therapy for patients suffering from leukemia and tumors. The inner bark of Pau d'Arco contains, amongst other things: lapachol (naphtaquinones), anthraquinones, xyloid, hydrobenzonic acid, and flavonoids (including quercetin, see 4.3).

Animal studies by the American National Cancer Institute have established that lapachol is active against cancer and tumors. However, the applied dose had to be so high that side effects were inevitable. The amount of lapachol present in Pau d'Arco preparations is insufficient to have a significant effect on cancer.

Pau d'Arco does, however, have important antibacterial, antiviral, fungicidal, anti-inflammatory and antiparasitical properties.

Milk thistle (Carduus marianus)

Milk thistle is especially important in the treatment of liver complaints. As a cancer remedy, therefore, it is mainly useful as a support in the treatment of liver cancer. In addition to this, it is an antioxidant which offers some protection against radiation.

Milk thistle's active ingredients are silymarin, amino acids, essential fatty acids, bitters, and essential oil. These are all responsible for a general stimulant effect on the liver, like the regeneration of liver cells, stimulating detoxification, stimulating gall production, reactivating the liver's functioning and the liver membranes. In addition, milk thistle generally protects the liver: as an antioxidant, it protects the liver's cell membranes against oxidation, toxins, and harmful digestive waste.

Licorice (Glycyrrhiza glabra)

Licorice root strongly stimulates the immune system. It contains, amongst others, glycyrrhizin, glabrinic acid, saponins, amino acids, enzymes, and several flavonoids. The active ingredients in licorice root have been shown to stimulate the thymus function and the production of interferon, and activate macrophages and killer cells. Licorice root's anti-tumor effect has been demonstrated scientifically. Licorice is also an antioxidant, especially protecting the liver from lipid peroxides. It has a soothing effect, particularly on the mucous membranes. Licorice may also be applied to stomach ulcers and diarrhoea, and has an anti-inflammatory, expectorant, and anti-allergenic effect. It also decreases the incidence of tumors.

Cat's claw (Uncaria tomentosa)

Cat's claw, a creeper, has been used by the Ashanica Indians for hundreds of years as a remedy for immune system and digestive disorders. Since the 1970's, scientific studies have take place in various countries to research the many applications of cat's claw. The herb has been demonstrated effective in case of cancer, arthritis, inflammation of the joints, herpes, shingles, allergies, ulcers, candidiasis, hormonal imbalance, environmental intoxications, AIDS, and infections of the gastrointestinal tract.
During a 1988 international conference for traditional medicine in Lima, Peru, the very encouraging results of the application of cat's claw in the treatment of 14 types of cancer in 700 patients were lectured on.
So far, the following active ingredients in cat's claw have been identified: six isolated oxindolic alkaloids, of which isopteropodin (isomer A) was

shown to have a highly stimulant effect on the phagocytosis (220-230%). Another component, rynchophylline, was demonstrated to counter platelet aggregation, which makes it a potential remedy against thrombosis and helpful for the prevention of infarcts. Triterpenes, beta-sisterol, stigmasterol en campesterol in cat's claw are responsible for the antioxidant, cell wall protecting, antiviral, anti-tumor and anti-inflammatory qualities of this herb.

Echinacea (Echinacea angustifolia)

Echinacea is an excellent remedy for infections, which stimulates the immune system. Echinacea activates white blood cells, has a depurative effect on the blood, is anti-inflammatory and antiseptic. The root is applied when resistance against infections is low, and to counter infections. Active ingredients are (amongst others) inulin, echinacoside, polysaccharides, phytosterols, resins, acetylenes, essential oils, betaine, caffeic acid, trihydroxyphenylproic acid and pentadecadine.

Chapter 5

Frequently Asked Questions About the Herbal Tea

Frequently Asked Questions About the Herbal Tea

Every day, dozens of questions arrive at Elaine Alexander's office from people all over the world who take Flor.Essence. Elaine's daughter Leslie and the Flora employees try as best they can to personally reply to as many people as possible and supply information. The most frequently asked question is, 'These are my symptoms or I was diagnosed as such; do you think the tea can help me?' That is a question the tea's manufacturer can not and may not answer, since the tea is not a registered medicine. The only information that may be shared is what the experiences of millions of other consumers have been in similar cases. Many have dedicated their experiences to paper, as you may read in the testimonials chapter (chapter 6). The answers to the questions in this chapter are based partly on the information supplied by the manufacturer and partly on the experiences of those who take the tea or have taken it.

Did the Ojibwa Indians know the exact effect of the herbs?

They probably didn't. The Indians didn't have access to the modern research technology available today. Their research method consisted of studying animals and of testing flavor and results. Even before 1900, they knew about the effects of the eight herbs in their environment, but of course that environment is substantially different from that which we live in today. In some areas perhaps the Indians would have been more knowledgeable than Westerners. For instance, the Indians had known for centuries that using the whole plant is more effective than just using its isolated components. Unfortunately, many documents about herbal medicine are lost forever, not just those concerning Indian medicine, but also documents by the Egyptians, Chinese, Arabs, and Greeks.

Why did Rene Caisse cease to inject the herbal mixture?

Only one herb, sheep sorrel, was ever injected. The other herbs were administered orally, as a decoction. The injections took place during the research period, when Rene and Dr. Fisher tried to determine the best way to achieve a maximum effect with the herb formula. The injections however were painful and unsuitable for certain cancer patients. And they necessitated visits to the clinic. Later, Dr. Brusch and Rene discovered that the eight herbs were most effective when taken together as a tea. After that, sheep sorrel was no longer injected.

Is it true that there are many similar products available?
This book describes the story of the eight-herb formula of the Ojibwa Indians, with which nurse Rene Caisse treated cancer patients for over 50 years. Later on, Dr. Charles A. Brusch and radio producer Elaine Alexander took over Rene's cause, until a suitable manufacturer was found in Flora Manufacturing & Distributing Ltd. at Burnaby, Canada. The tea marketed under the brand name Flor.Essence, produced by Flora and with Elaine Alexander's signature on the packaging, is the tea this book is about. From the very first moment when Rene Caisse attracted publicity, several variations have been marketed by other parties. Marketed as 'the original Ojibwa formula', 'Rene Caisse's tea', and other such names, it was always claimed that these were 'the one and only real tea'. The best-known variation is the four-herb formula Essiac, which contains four of the eight herbs that make up Rene Caisse's tea. Essiac was brought on the market after Rene handed over part of the herb formula to David Fingard of the Resperin Company (see chapter 2.2, 1977).

Why is it some people have less than one litre of tea after preparation?
Often, people use an oversize pot, or forget to put the lid on, thus losing more liquid through evaporation than strictly necessary. Also, be careful the mixture doesn't boil over, because that would spoil the proportions, which are essential to the effectiveness of the tea.

Why does the tea have to be prepared according to such a specific procedure?
We call it a herbal tea, but really we're talking about an extract. Its preparation differs from that of ordinary tea. The herbs require a longer

time to release their active ingredients. Especially when a plant's root or bark are used, boiling is essential to extract the active ingredients. For this reason, the eight-herb mixture is not available in tea bags, and the mixture should be left to stand at room temperature for 10-12 hours during preparation. The 20-minute wait after boiling up the mixture is needed to allow the herbs to sink to the bottom of the pot, leaving as clear a liquid as possible.

Why is the ready-made product so much more expensive?

Preparation of the tea is a labor-intensive process and transporting the bottles is much more expensive than transporting the dried herb mixture. The liquid product and the dried mixture are equally effective (see appendix IV).

Can the tea be taken during hospitalization?

Certainly. During a stay in hospital, it may be easier to use the ready-made, bottled variety. The bottles may be kept in the hospital fridge. But you can also have someone prepare the tea for you at home and bring it in for you. Discuss with the nursing staff how much of the tea you would like to take and when. If you meet with lack of understanding or cooperation, tell them it's just a herbal tea that you feel better for taking. Doctors and nursing staff may contact the importer for more information. For patients in isolation the dried mixture is preferable, prepared by the nursing staff. Consult with them about the preparation.

How can patients who are unable to drink the herbal tea still ingest it?

The tea may not be administered through an drip, but may be applied directly to the stomach through a tube. The tea may also be given to a patient with a pipette, ideally underneath the tongue. If the flavor is a problem, the tea may be mixed with another (sugar-free) drink.

Why should the tea be taken on an empty stomach?

Because that way, it is absorbed more quickly and more completely. You don't necessarily have to take the tea either before breakfast in the morning or before you go to bed in the evening. Maybe you would prefer another moment of the day, when your stomach is also empty. Even if you can't take the tea on an empty stomach, it is still useful to take the tea.

How quickly can you expect results?

Don't compare the tea's effect to that of other medicines. The effect of the herbs is mild, thorough, and slow. Some users experience spectaculair improvement after just two weeks; others don't notice any change for several months. Starting from a healthy situation, it will probably take several weeks for the tea to have a noticeable effect. When you have been suffering from complaints for a prolonged period of time, you may expect the tea to take a longer time also before it is effective.

Are there any known side effects?

No. There are no side effects to using the tea. But you should be aware that the tea has a detoxifying effect. Possible symptoms like headaches, fatigue, or spots, are indications of detoxification. Continued use of the tea will see these complaints disappear. And not every user suffers these symptoms. It is recommended you drink plenty of water (about 2 litres a day) while you are taking the tea, to remove the toxins as quickly as possible. If you are suffering from headaches, it may help to (temporarily) stop using dairy products and take a vitamin B supplement. You may also lower the dosage of the tea.

Why shouldn't the tea be used during pregnancy?

When you're pregnant, your body may react differently to herbs, especially if you are using them for a longer period of time. Also, some of the herbs in the formula should not be used during pregnancy, for instance because they are slightly diuretic, because they contain certain acids, or because they have a stimulating effect on the uterus. Despite the fact that the dose of each herb is quite low, using the tea during pregnancy is advised against, to prevent the occurrence of undesirable effects.

The tea stimulates the appetite, but that is not an effect desired by all, isn't it?
Especially those who are ill write or relate that their appetite improved as a result of using the tea. For patients who have suffered weight loss as a result of their illness, and who lack appetite, that is a desirable effect. Many users who already had a healthy appetite, experience a decreased craving for sweets and less inclination to binge.

If the tea is used in conjunction with other medication or therapies, won't those drugs be expelled as toxins?
The herbal mixture stimulates the immune system to make a distinction between good and bad cells in the body. Only cells that have mutated wrongly, have been toxicated, or have died, are recognized as such and removed. Medicines or chemotherapy aren't cells. So, using the tea doesn't interfere with any other kind of medication. On the contrary, experience has shown that side effects of allopathic medication may be diminished as a result of using the tea.

If the tea is used at the same time as a dietary supplement, don't you ingest too much of certain substances?
Although each individual herb is rich in vitamins, minerals and other nutrients, the amount you ingest of those after dilution is very minimal. The risk of excessive application when combined with a nutritional supplement is therefore nonexistent. It is even recommended you take a nutritional supplement during the detoxification process, to prevent deficiencies (see chapter 1.2) and to support specific bodily functions.

In what way does the body get rid of toxins?
Usually, users of the detoxifying tea find waste matter in the toilet bowl. This may consist of slimy, bloody or other waste products. The discharge of toxins may also lead to a differently colored stool. The bowels, after all, are the most appropriate channel for discharge, and in many cases will also

prove the nearest exit. But there are also cases where the body chose other exits, like skin, nose, and even eyes and ears. The occasional user has reported old scars opening up to discharge waste matter. To this date, two users have reported a dark liquid running from their eyes for several hours. Several times, moles have opened up, mass underneath was discharged, and the skin healed itself again afterwards.

If you wish to temporarily stop taking the tea, is that OK?

For healthy people, an occasional period of rest is an excellent idea. For instance, you may stop taking the tea for a week after each pack, or after each month of taking the tea. Such a pause even improves the absorption of the tea when you start using it again. However, in case of illness it is recommended you keep taking the tea on a daily basis, to prevent deterioration of your condition.

What is the appropriate dose for dogs and cats?

The manufacturer supplies a guideline, but the exact dosage is best determined individually. Depending on your pet's weight, you may administer daily: up to 2,5 kg., 1-1,5 tablespoons; up to 8 kg., 2 tbsp.; up to 15 kg., 2-4 tbsp.; up to 30 kg., 4-6 tbsp.; up to 60 kg., 6-8 tbsp.; over 60 kg., twice a day 8-12 tbsp. The daily dose may be divided up in two portions, preferably administered on an empty stomach. That may be done very easily with the aid of a pipette. If that is a problem you, may mix up the tea in your pets food. If complaints lessen, and your pets condition is stable, you may start giving the tea three times a week rather than every day.

Chapter 6

Testimonials

Testimonials

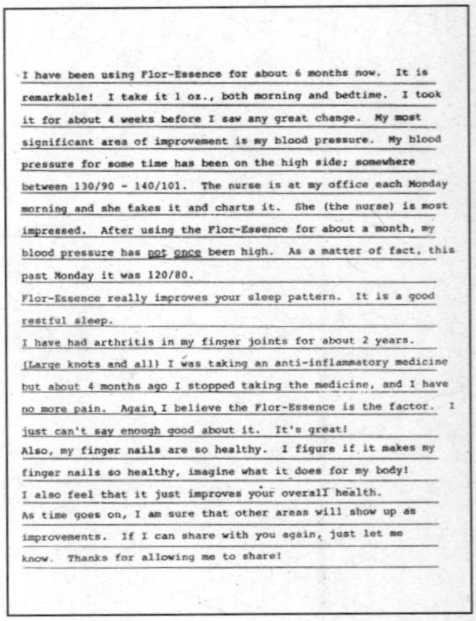

I have been using Flor-Essence for about 6 months now. It is remarkable! I take it 1 oz., both morning and bedtime. I took it for about 4 weeks before I saw any great change. My most significant area of improvement is my blood pressure. My blood pressure for some time has been on the high side; somewhere between 130/90 - 140/101. The nurse is at my office each Monday morning and she takes it and charts it. She (the nurse) is most impressed. After using the Flor-Essence for about a month, my blood pressure has not once been high. As a matter of fact, this past Monday it was 120/80.
Flor-Essence really improves your sleep pattern. It is a good restful sleep.
I have had arthritis in my finger joints for about 2 years. (Large knots and all) I was taking an anti-inflammatory medicine but about 4 months ago I stopped taking the medicine, and I have no more pain. Again, I believe the Flor-Essence is the factor. I just can't say enough good about it. It's great!
Also, my finger nails are so healthy. I figure if it makes my finger nails so healthy, imagine what it does for my body!
I also feel that it just improves your overall health.
As time goes on, I am sure that other areas will show up as improvements. If I can share with you again, just let me know. Thanks for allowing me to share!

Arthritis / High blood pressure

I have been using Flor.Essence for about 6 months now. It is remarkable! I take it 1 oz., both morning and bedtime. I took it for about 4 weeks before I saw any great change. My most significant area of improvement is my blood pressure. My blood pressure for some time has been on the high side: somewhere between 130/90 - 140/101. The nurse is at my office each Monday morning and she takes it and charts it. She (the nurse) is most impressed. After using the Flor.Essence for about a month, my blood pressure has not once been high. As a matter of fact, this past Monday it was 120/80. Flor.Essence really improves your sleep pattern. It is a good restful sleep. I have had arthritis in my finger joints for about 2 years. (Large knots and all) I was taking an anti-inflammatory medicine but about 4 months ago I stopped taking the medicine, and I have no more pain. Again, I believe the Flor.Essence is the factor. I just can't say enough good about it. It's great!
Also, my finger nails are so healthy. I figure if it makes my finger nails so healthy, imagine what it does for my body!
I also feel that it just improves your overall health. As time goes on, I am sure that other areas will show up as improvements. If I can share with you again, just let me know. Thanks for allowing me to share!

M.B. Montana, USA

SEX female
AGE
DIAGNOSIS high blood pressure
DATE arthritic for 2 years

CONDITION, COMPLAINTS
knots in finger joints, pain

MEDICATION OR TREATMENT
anti-inflammatory medicine until 4 months ago

HAS BEEN USING FLOR.ESSENCE SINCE
6 months ago

RESULTS AFTER
4 weeks

CONSISTING OF
blood pressure back to normal
no more arthritis pain
improved sleep
healthier fingernails
generally improved health

Old birth material in uterus

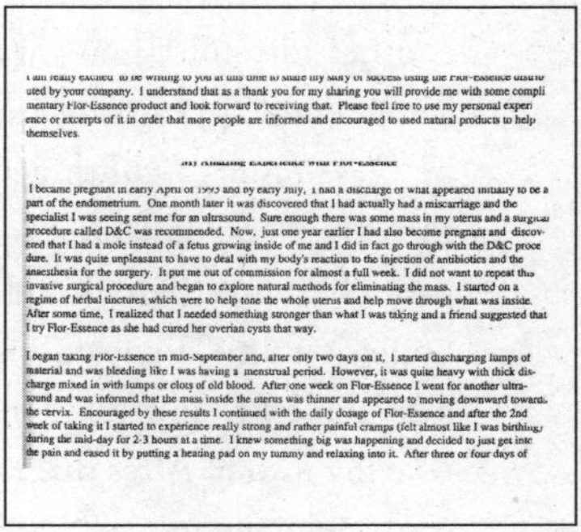
I am really excited to be writing to you at this time to share my story of success using the Flor-Essence distributed by your company. I understand that as a thank you for my sharing you will provide me with some complimentary Flor-Essence product and look forward to receiving that. Please feel free to use my personal experience or excerpts of it in order that more people are informed and encouraged to used natural products to help themselves.

My Amazing Experience with Flor-Essence

I became pregnant in early April of 1993 and by early July, I had a discharge of what appeared initially to be a part of the endometrium. One month later it was discovered that I had actually had a miscarriage and the specialist I was seeing sent me for an ultrasound. Sure enough there was some mass in my uterus and a surgical procedure called D&C was recommended. Now, just one year earlier I had also become pregnant and discovered that I had a mole instead of a fetus growing inside of me and I did in fact go through with the D&C procedure. It was quite unpleasant to have to deal with my body's reaction to the injection of antibiotics and the anaesthesia for the surgery. It put me out of commission for almost a full week. I did not want to repeat this invasive surgical procedure and began to explore natural methods for eliminating the mass. I started on a regime of herbal tinctures which were to help tone the whole uterus and help move through what was inside. After some time, I realized that I needed something stronger than what I was taking and a friend suggested that I try Flor-Essence as she had cured her overian cysts that way.

I began taking Flor-Essence in mid-September and, after only two days on it, I started discharging lumps of material and was bleeding like I was having a menstrual period. However, it was quite heavy with thick discharge mixed in with lumps or clots of old blood. After one week on Flor-Essence I went for another ultrasound and was informed that the mass inside the uterus was thinner and appeared to moving downward towards the cervix. Encouraged by these results I continued with the daily dosage of Flor-Essence and after the 2nd week of taking it I started to experience really strong and rather painful cramps (felt almost like I was birthing) during the mid-day for 2-3 hours at a time. I knew something big was happening and decided to just get into the pain and eased it by putting a heating pad on my tummy and relaxing into it. After three or four days of

I am really excited to be writing to you at this time to share my story of success using the Flor.Essence distributed by your company. I understand that as a thank you for my sharing you will provide me with some complimentary Flor.Essence product and look forward to receiving that. Please feel free to use my personal experience or excerpts of it in order that more people are informed and encouraged to use natural products to help themselves.

My amazing experience with Flor.Essence:

I became pregnant in early April of 1993 and by early July, I had a discharge of what appeared initially to be a part of the endometrium. One month later it was discovered that I had actually had a miscarriage and the specialist I was seeing sent me for an ultrasound. Sure enough there was some mass in my uterus and a surgical procedure called D & C was recommended. Now, just one year earlier I had also become pregnant and discovered that I had a mole instead of a fetus growing inside of me and I did in fact go through with the D & C procedure. It was quite unpleasant to have to deal with my body's reaction to the injection of antibiotics and the anaesthesia for the surgery. It put me out of commission for almost a full week. I did not want to repeat this invasive surgical procedure and began te explore natural methods for eliminating the mass. I started on a regime of herbal tinctures which were to help tone the whole uterus and help move through what was inside. After some time, I realized that I needed something stronger than what I was taking and a friend suggested that I try Flor.Essence as she had cured her overian cysts that way.

I began taking Flor.Essence in mid-September and, after only two days on it, I started discharging lumps of material and was bleeding like I was having a menstrual period. However, it was quite heavy with thick discharge mixed with lumps or clots of old blood. After one week on Flor.Essence I went for another ultrasound and was informed that the mass inside the uterus was thinner and appeared to moving downward towards the cervix. Encouraged by these results I continued with the daily dosage of Flor.Essence and after the 2nd week of taking it I started to experience really strong and rather painful cramps (felt almost like I was birthing) during the mid-day for 2-3 hours at a time. I knew something big was happening and decided to just get into the pain and eased it by putting a heating pad on my tummy and relaxing into it. After three or four days of these intense cramps I went to the washroom and out slipped a mass of old birth material which was rougly the size of a tampon. Immediately after discharging this piece of material the bleeding subsided and by the next day I was no longer bleeding. Deep inside I was convinced that everything was now cleared up and thought that another ultrasound was in order to confirm this. We were in the process of moving out of the city when all of this was happening, so after having had a chance to settle a bit I arranged to have a third ultrasound and have heard just today, October 15, 1993, that my uterus is now back to normal and nothing further needs to be done. Can't tell you how relieved and thankful I am for Flor.Essence.

Thank you again for your support in my sharing this experience with you.

Very sincerely yours,

L.P., Vancouver Canada
October 1993

SEX female
AGE
DIAGNOSIS old birth material in uterus
DATE april 1992

CONDITION, COMPLAINTS
operation, treatment with antibiotics
miscarriage in april 1993
mass of old tissue in uterus

MEDICATION OR TREATMENT
various natural remedies to cleanse the uterus

HAS BEEN USING FLOR.ESSENCE SINCE
september 1993

RESULTS AFTER
2 days

CONSISTING OF
bleeding with lumps of old material
mass inside uterus became thinner
strong cramps after 2 weeks and discharge of old birth material
uterus clean in October 1993

DETAILS
Flor.Essence had been recommended by a friend who had been cured of ovarian cysts by taking the tea

Breast cancer

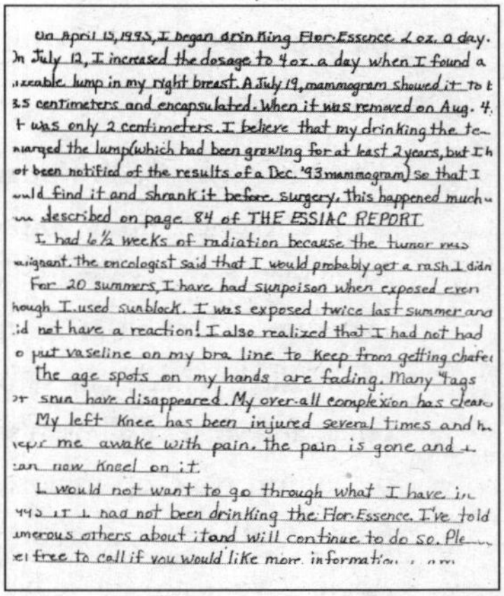
On April 15, 1995, I began drinking Flor.Essence 2 oz. a day.
n July 12, I increased the dosage to 4 oz. a day when I found a
izeable lump in my right breast. A July 19, mammogram showed it to b
3.5 centimeters and encapsulated. When it was removed on Aug. 4,
t was only 2 centimeters. I believe that my drinking the te
nlarged the lump (which had been growing for at least 2 years, but I h
ot been notified of the results of a Dec. '93 mammogram) so that I
ould find it and shrank it before surgery. this happened much
described on page 84 of THE ESSIAC REPORT
I had 6 1/2 weeks of radiation because the tumor was
alignant. the oncologist said that I would probably get a rash. I didn
For 20 summers, I have had sunpoison when exposed even
hough I used sunblock. I was exposed twice last summer and
id not have a reaction! I also realized that I had not had
o put vaseline on my bra line to keep from getting chafe
the age spots on my hands are fading. Many 'tags
of skin have disappeared. My over-all complexion has clear
My left knee has been injured several times and h
kept me awake with pain. the pain is gone and I
can now kneel on it.
I would not want to go through what I have in
1995 if I had not been drinking the Flor.Essence. I've told
umerous others about it and will continue to do so. Ple
eel free to call if you would like more information

On April 15, 1995, I began drinking Flor.Essence 2 oz a day. On July 12, I increased the dosage to 4 oz. A day when I found a sizeable lump in my right breast. A July 19 mammogram showed it to be 3.5 centimetres and encapsulated. When it was removed on Aug. 4, it was only 2 centimetres. I believe my drinking the tea enlarged the lump (which had been growing for at least 2 years but I had not been notified of the results of a Dec.'93 mammogram) so that I could find it, and shrank it before surgery, this happened such as you described on page 84 of the Essiac Report.

I had 6 1/2 weeks of radiation because the tumor was malignant. The oncologist said that I would probably get a rash. I didn't. For 20 summers, I have had sunpoisoning when exposed even though I used sunblock. I was exposed twice last summer and did not have a reaction! I also realized that I had not had to put vaseline on my bra line to keep from getting chafed. The age spots on my hands are fading. Many 'tags' of skin have disappeared. My overall complexion has cleared. My left knee has been injured several times and has kept me awake with pain. The pain is gone and I can now kneel on it.

I would not want to go through what I have in 1995 if I had not been drinking the Flor.Essence. I've told numerous others about it and will continue to do so. Please feel free to call if you would like more information. I am 57 years old.

E.C. B., Florida USA
november 1995

SEX	female
AGE	57 years
DIAGNOSIS	breast cancer
DATE	July 1995

CONDITION, COMPLAINTS
tumor 3.5 cm. in size

MEDICATION OR TREATMENT
radiotherapy for 6 1/2 weeks
operation August 1995

HAS BEEN USING FLOR.ESSENCE SINCE
April 1995

RESULTS AFTER
3 months

CONSISTING OF
growth and encapsulation of tumor, followed by shrinking to 2 cm. at time of operation
in addition, no longer susceptible to sun poisoning, many 'tags' of skin disappeared, chronic knee pain disappeared.

Bone cancer

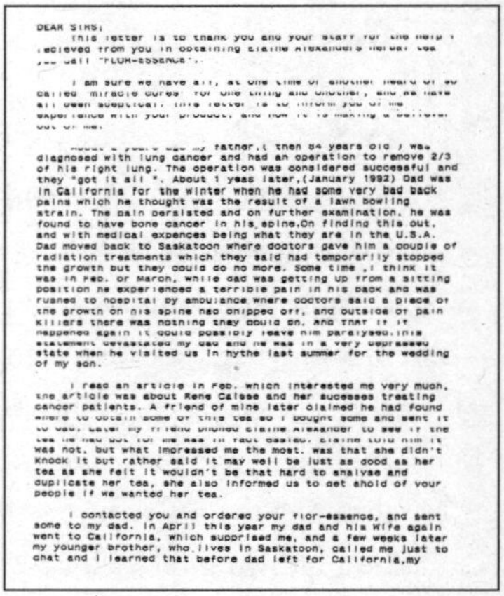
DEAR SIRS;
This letter is to thank you and your staff for the help I recieved from you in obtaining Elaine Alexanders herbal tea you call "FLOR-ESSENCE".

I am sure we have all, at one time or another heard of so called 'miracle cures' for one thing and another, and we have all been sceptical. This letter is to inform you of my experiance with your product, and how it is making a believer out of me.

[illegible] father,(then 84 years old) was diagnosed with lung cancer and had an operation to remove 2/3 of his right lung. The operation was considered successful and they "got it all ". About 1 yeas later,(January 1992) Dad was in California for the winter when he had some very bad back pains which he thought was the result of a lawn bowling strain. The pain persisted and on further examination, he was found to have bone cancer in his spine.On finding this out, and with medical expences being what they are in the U.S.A. Dad moved back to Saskatoon where doctors gave him a couple of radiation treatments which they said had temporarily stopped the growth but they could do no more. Some time ,I think it was in Feb. or March, while dad was getting up from a sitting position he experienced a terrible pain in his back and was rushed to hospital by ambulance where doctors said a piece of the growth on his spine had chipped off, and outside of pain killers there was nothing they could do, and that if it happened again it could possibly leave him paralysed.This statement devastated my dad and he was in a very depressed state when he visited us in hythe last summer for the wedding of my son.

I read an article in Feb. which interested me very much, the article was about Rene Caisse and her sucesses treating cancer patients. A friend of mine later claimed he had found where to obtain some of this tea so I bought some and sent it to dad. Later my friend phoned Elaine Alexander to see if the tea he had got for me was in fact essiac. Elaine told him it was not, but what impressed me the most, was that she didn't knock it but rather said it may well be just as good as her tea as she felt it wouldn't be that hard to analyse and duplicate her tea, she also informed us to get ahold of your people if we wanted her tea.

I contacted you and ordered your flor-essence, and sent some to my dad. In April this year my dad and his Wife again went to California, which supprised me, and a few weeks later my younger brother, who lives in Saskatoon, called me just to chat and I learned that before dad left for California,my

This letter is to thank you and your staff for the help I received from you in obtaining Elaine Alexanders herbal tea you call 'Flor.Essence'.
I am sure we have all, at one time or another heard of so called 'miracle cures' for one thing and another, and we have all been sceptical. This letter is to inform you of my experience with your product, and how it is making a believer out of me.
About 2 years ago my father (then 84 years old) was diagnosed with lung cancer and had an operation to remove 2/3 of his right lung. The operation was considered successful and they 'got it all'. About 1 year later (January 1992) Dad was in California for the winter when he had some very bad back pains which he thought was the result of a lawn bowling strain. The pain persisted and on further examination, he was found to have bone cancer in his spine. On finding this out, and with the medical expences being what they are in the U.S.A., Dad moved back to Sakatoon where doctors gave him a couple of radiation treatments which they said had temporarily stopped the growth but they could do no more. Some time, I think it was in Feb. or March, while Dad was getting up from a sitting position he experienced a terrible pain in his back and was rushed to hospital by ambulance where doctors said a piece of the growth on his spine had chipped off, and outside of pain killers there was nothing they could do, and if it happened again it could possibly leave him paralysed. This statement devastated my dad and he was in a very depressed state when he visited us in hythe last summer for the wedding of my son. I read an article in Feb. which interested me very much, the article was about Rene Caisse and her successes treating cancer patients. A friend of mine later claimed he had found where to obtain some of this tea so I bought some and sent it to dad. Later my friend phoned Elaine Alexander to see if the tea he had got for me was in fact essiac. Elaine told him it was not, but what interested me the most, was that she didn't knock it but rather said it may well be just as good as her tea as she felt it wouldn't be that hard to analyse and duplicate her tea, she also

informed us to get ahold of your people if we wanted her tea. I contacted you and ordered your Flor.Essence, and sent some to my dad. In April this year my dad and his wife again went to California, which surprised me, and a few weeks later my younger brother, who lives in Saskatoon, called me just to chat and I learned that before dad left for California, my brother had taken him to 2 different doctors for a check up and they could find no sign of the cancer. By the way Dad plans to be up to visit us in June which is a trip I never thought I'd see him make again. There's more too. I gathered all the information I could find on Rene Caisse and in reading one of the articles where a doctor had taken a terminally ill cancer patient, who also had diabetes, to her and she not only overcame the cancer but also the diabetes. I took that article to a friend of mine in Grande Prairie who had contracted diabeted some 2 years previously and he immediately went to the health food store in the mail and bought some. About 3 weeks later he informed me that he had gone from 40 units a day to 28 units. I must admit, this doesn't mean much to me as I don't know what a unit is, but it sounded like we were on the right track. A couple of weeks later I was attending a meeting that my friend was also at and he said 'this is the eighth day I haven't taken any insulin' and said he had gone for a check-up and his doctor said he had only ever heard of this once before and couldn't explain it. I asked my friend if he had told the doctor about drinking the Flor.Essence and he said 'no, he wouldn't believe me anyway'. To date he is just over 7 weeks off his insulin. Since talking to you on the phone I found out that my friend had recommended your Flor.Essence to another diabetic friend who after three weeks was starting to have a reaction from his insulin shots. I will keep you posted on this case and many others I have since given or recommended your Flor.Essence to.

Thanks once again for all your help and a wonderful product.

signed, 'a believer', G.S. Alberta, USA, May 1993

SEX	male
AGE	84 years
DIAGNOSIS	lung cancer
DATE	1991

had an operation
bone cancer in spine, January 1992
piece of growth on spine chipped off March 1992

CONDITION, COMPLAINTS
pain; apart from painkillers there's nothing doctors can do

MEDICATION OR TREATMENT
painkillers

HAS BEEN USING FLOR.ESSENCE SINCE
imitation tea since February 1993
a little later changed to Flor.Essence

RESULTS AFTER
3 months

CONSISTING OF
no lunger suffers from cancer

DETAILS
diabetic friend had stopped taking insulin after having taken Flor.Essence for several weeks. Another diabetic friend who had started taking Flor.Essence developed a reaction to his insulin injections.

Colitis ulcerosa

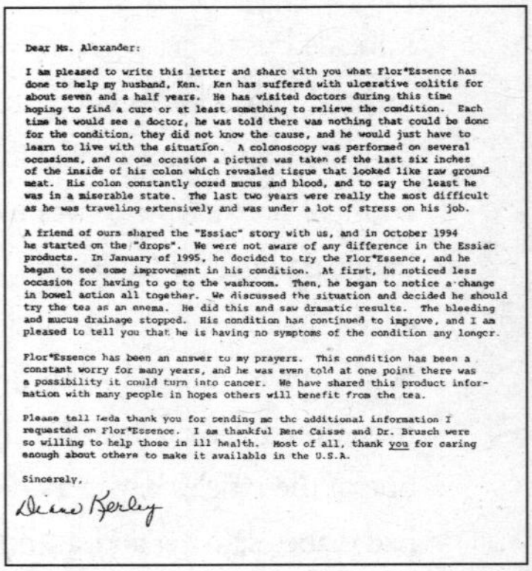

Dear Ms. Alexander:

I am pleased to write this letter and share with you what Flor*Essence has done to help my husband, Ken. Ken has suffered with ulcerative colitis for about seven and a half years. He has visited doctors during this time hoping to find a cure or at least something to relieve the condition. Each time he would see a doctor, he was told there was nothing that could be done for the condition, they did not know the cause, and he would just have to learn to live with the situation. A colonoscopy was performed on several occasions, and on one occasion a picture was taken of the last six inches of the inside of his colon which revealed tissue that looked like raw ground meat. His colon constantly oozed mucus and blood, and to say the least he was in a miserable state. The last two years were really the most difficult as he was traveling extensively and was under a lot of stress on his job.

A friend of ours shared the "Essiac" story with us, and in October 1994 he started on the "drops". We were not aware of any difference in the Essiac products. In January of 1995, he decided to try the Flor*Essence, and he began to see some improvement in his condition. At first, he noticed less occasion for having to go to the washroom. Then, he began to notice a change in bowel action all together. We discussed the situation and decided he should try the tea as an enema. He did this and saw dramatic results. The bleeding and mucus drainage stopped. His condition has continued to improve, and I am pleased to tell you that he is having no symptoms of the condition any longer.

Flor*Essence has been an answer to my prayers. This condition has been a constant worry for many years, and he was even told at one point there was a possibility it could turn into cancer. We have shared this product information with many people in hopes others will benefit from the tea.

Please tell Leda thank you for sending me the additional information I requested on Flor*Essence. I am thankful Rene Caisse and Dr. Brusch were so willing to help those in ill health. Most of all, thank you for caring enough about others to make it available in the U.S.A.

Sincerely,

Diane Kerley

I am pleased to write this letter and share with you what Flor.Essence has done to help my husband, Ken. Ken has suffered with ulcerative colitis for about seven and a half years. He has visited doctors during this time hoping to find a cure or at least something to relieve the condition. Each time he would see a doctor, he was told there was nothing that could be done for the condition, they did not know the cause, and he would just have to learn to live with the situation. A colonoscopy was performed on several occasions, and on one occasion a picture was taken of the last six inches of the inside of his colon which revealed tissue that looked like raw ground meat. His colon constantly oozed mucus and blood, and to say the least he was in a miserable state. The last two years were really the most difficult as he was traveling extensively and was under a lot of stress on his job.

A friend of ours shared the 'Essiac' story with us, and in October 1994 he started on the 'drops'. We were not aware of any difference in the Essiac products. In January of 1995, he decided to try the Flor.Essence, and he began to see some improvement in his condition. At first he noticed less occasion for having to go to the washroom. Then, he began to notice a change in bowel action all together. We discussed the situation and decided he should try the tea as an enema. He did this and saw dramatic results. The bleeding and mucus drainage stopped. His condition has continued to improve, and I am pleased to tell you that he is having no

SEX	male
AGE	
DIAGNOSIS	colitis ulcerosa
DATE	late 1993

CONDITION, COMPLAINTS
blood and mucus in stool
in a miserable state

MEDICATION OR TREATMENT
doctors claimed nothing could be done

HAS BEEN USING FLOR.ESSENCE SINCE
Essiac since October 1994
Flor.Essence since January 1995

RESULTS AFTER
-

CONSISTING OF
less occasion for having to go to washroom, change in bowel action
used tea as an enema, after which bleeding and mucus drainage stopped
no longer any symptoms

DETAILS
had been suffering from this condition for as long as 7 1/2 years

symptoms of the condition any longer.

Flor.Essence has been an answer to my prayers. This condition has been a constant worry for many years, and he was even told there was a possibility it could turn into cancer. We have shared this product information with many people in hopes others will benefit from the tea.

Please tell Leda thank you for sending me the additional information I requested on Flor.Essence. I am thankful Rene Caisse and Dr. Brusch were so willing to help those in ill health. Most af all, thank you for caring enough about others to make it available in the U.S.A.

Sincerely,
D.K.
may 1995

Bowel problems

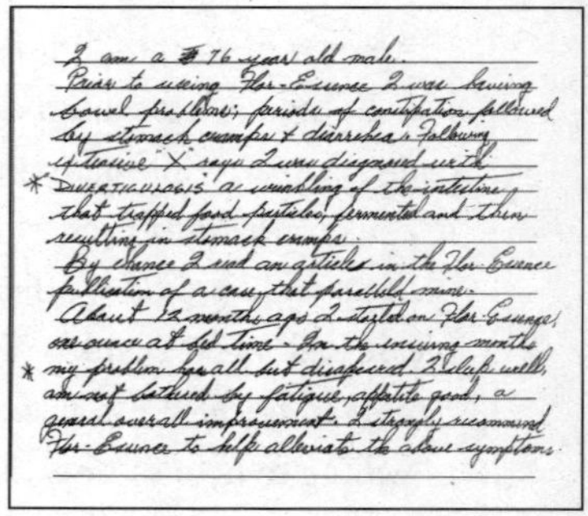
I am a # 76 year old male.
Prior to using Flor-Essence I was having
bowel problems; periods of constipation followed
by stomach cramps & diarrhea. Following
extensive X rays I was diagnosed with
* DIVERTICULOSIS a wrinkling of the intestine
that trapped food particles, fermented and then
resulting in stomach cramps.
By chance I read an article in the Flor-Essence
publication of a case that paralleled mine.
About 12 months ago I started on Flor-Essence,
one ounce at bed time. In the insuing months
* my problem has all but disapeared. I sleep well,
am not bothered by fatigue, appetite good, a
general overall improvement. I strongly recommend
Flor-Essence to help alleviate the above symptoms.

I am a 76 year old male.
Prior to using Flor.Essence I was having bowel problems: periods of constipation followed by stomach cramps & diarrhea. Following extensive 'X' rays I was diagnosed with Diverticulosis, a wrinkling of the intestine that trapped food particles, fermented and then resulting in stomach cramps.
By chance I read an article in the Flor.Essence publication of a case that paralleled mine. About 12 months ago I started on Flor.Essence, one ounce at bed time. In the insuing months my problem has all but disappeared. I sleep well, am not bothered by fatigue, appetite good, a general overall improvement. I strongly recommend Flor.Essence to help alleviate the above symptoms.

G.W.

SEX	male
AGE	76 years
DIAGNOSIS	diverticulosis (wrinkling of the intestine)
DATE	

CONDITION, COMPLAINTS
constipation, followed by stomach cramps and diarrhea

MEDICATION OR TREATMENT
-

HAS BEEN USING FLOR.ESSENCE SINCE
June 1994

RESULTS AFTER
several months

CONSISTING OF
hardly any complaints left
sleeps better, less tired
good appetite
general overall improvement

Hepatitis C

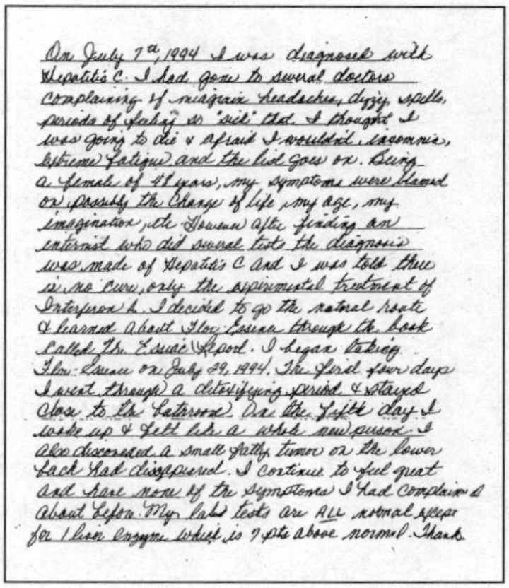
On July 7th, 1994 I was diagnosed with
Hepatitis C. I had gone to several doctors
complaining of migraine headaches, dizzy spells,
periods of feeling so "sick" that I thought I
was going to die & afraid I wouldn't, insomnia,
extreme fatigue and the list goes on. Being
a female of 48 years, my symptoms were blamed
on possibly the change of life, my age, my
imagination, etc. However after finding an
internist who did several tests the diagnosis
was made of Hepatitis C and I was told there
is no cure, only the experimental treatment of
Interferon A. I decided to go the natural route
& learned about Flor-Essence through the book
called The Essiac Report. I began taking
Flor-Essence on July 29, 1994. The first four days
I went through a detoxifying period & stayed
close to the bathroom. On the fifth day I
woke up & felt like a whole new person. I
also discovered a small fatty tumor on the lower
back had disappeared. I continue to feel great
and have none of the symptoms I had complained
about before. My lab tests are ALL normal except
for 1 liver enzyme which is 7 pts above normal. Thank

On July 7th, 1994 I was diagnosed with Hepatitis C. I had gone to several doctors complaining of migraine headaches, dizzy spells, periods of feeling so 'sick' that I thought I was going to die and afraid I wouldn't, insomnia, extreme fatigue, and the list goes on. Being a female of 48 years, my symptoms were blamed on possibly the change of life, my age, my imagination, etc. However, after finding an internist who did several tests, the diagnosis was made of Hepatitis C and I was told there is no cure, only the experimental treatment of Interferon A. I decided to go the natural route and I learned about Flor.Essence on July 29, 1994. The first four days I went through a detoxifying period and stayed close to the bathroom. On the fifth day I woke up and felt like a whole new person. I also discovered a small fatty tumor on the lower back had disappeared. I continue to feel great and have none of the symptoms I had complained about before. My lab tests are ALL normal except for one liver enzyme which is 7 points above normal.

Thank you for this wonderful product.

R.L. J. Texas, USA
january 1995

SEX	female
AGE	48 years
DIAGNOSIS	hepatitis C
DATE	7 July 1994

CONDITION, COMPLAINTS
migraine headaches, dizzy spells, sickness, insomnia, extreme fatigue, etc.

MEDICATION OR TREATMENT
-

HAS BEEN USING FLOR.ESSENCE SINCE
29 July 1994

RESULTS AFTER
4 days

CONSISTING OF
a lot of bowel motion
after 5 days felt like a new person
no more symptoms, all lab tests normal
except for one liver enzyme 7 points above normal

DETAILS
a small fatty tumor on the lower back has also disappeared

Brain tumor

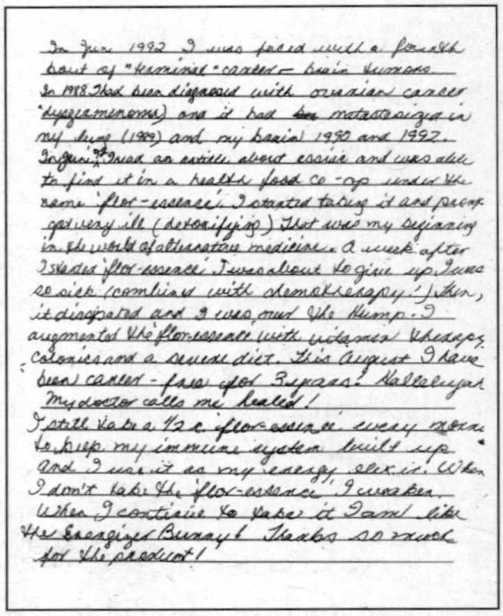
In June 1992 I was faced with a fourth
bout of "terminal" cancer – brain tumors.
In 1988 I had been diagnosed with ovarian cancer
(dysgermenoma) and it had metastesized in
my lung (1989) and my brain 1990 and 1992.
In June 92 I read an article about essiac and was able
to find it in a health food co-op under the
name 'flor-essence'. I started taking it and promp
got very ill (detoxifying) That was my beginning
in the world of alternative medicine. A week after
I started 'flor-essence' I was about to give up. I was
so sick (combined with chemotherapy!) Then,
it dissipated and I was over the hump. I
augmented the 'flor-essence' with vitamin therapy,
colonics and a severe diet. This August I have
been cancer-free for 3 years! Hallelujah
My doctor calls me healed!
I still take a 1/2 c. 'flor-essence' every morn
to keep my immune system built up
and I use it as my energy elixir. When
I don't take the 'flor-essence' I weaken.
When I continue to take it I am like
the Energizer Bunny! Thanks so much
for the product!

In June 1992, I was faced with a fourth bout of 'terminal' cancer - brain tumors. In 1988 I had been diagnosed with ovarian cancer (dysgermenoma) and it had metastesized in my lung (1989) and my brain (1990 and 1992). In June 1992 I read an article about Essiac and was able to find it in a health food co-op under the name 'flor.essence'. I started taking it and promptly got very ill (detoxifying). That was my beginning in the world of alternative medicine. A week after I started 'flor.essence' I was about to give up. I was so sick (combined with chemotherapy!). Then, it disappeared and I was over the hump. I augmented the 'flor.essence' with vitamin therapy, colonics and a severe diet. This august I have been cancer-free for 3 years! Hallelujah! My doctor calls me healed!

I still take a 1/2 c. 'flor.essence' every morning to help my immune system built up and I use it as my energy elexir. When I don't take the 'flor.essence' I weaken. When I continue to take it I am like Energizer Bunny! Thanks so much for the product!

Regards,
M.V., Ontario
august 1995

SEX	female
AGE	
DIAGNOSIS	ovarian cancer
DATE	1988

CONDITION, COMPLAINTS
cancer metastesized in lung 1989, in brain 1990 and 1992

MEDICATION OR TREATMENT
chemotherapy, vitamins, severe diet, colonics

HAS BEEN USING FLOR.ESSENCE SINCE
June 1992

RESULTS AFTER
1 week

CONSISTING OF
initially strong signs of detoxification, after that, improvement
free from cancer in 1992
still cancer-free 3 years later
increased energy.

DETAILS
weakens if stops taking Flor.Essence

Skin cancer

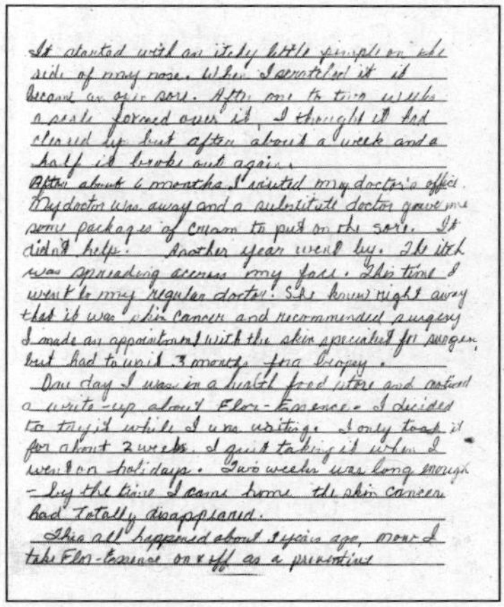
It started with an itchy little pimple on the side of my nose. When I scratched it it became an open sore. After one to two weeks a scale formed over it, I thought it had cleared up but after about a week and a half it broke out again.
After about 6 months I visited my doctor's office. My doctor was away and a substitute doctor gave me some packages of cream to put on the sore. It didn't help. Another year went by. The itch was spreading across my face. This time I went to my regular doctor. She knew right away that it was skin cancer and recommended surgery. I made an appointment with the skin specialist for surgery but had to wait 3 months for a biopsy.
One day I was in a health food store and noticed a write-up about Flor-Essence. I decided to try it while I was waiting. I only took it for about 2 weeks. I quit taking it when I went on holidays. Two weeks was long enough - by the time I came home the skin cancer had totally disappeared.
This all happened about 3 years ago, now I take Flor-Essence on & off as a preventive

It started with an itchy little pimple on the side of my nose. When I scratched it, it became an open sore. After one to two weeks a scale formed over it, I thought it had cleared up, but after about a week and a half it broke out again.

After about 6 months I visited my doctor's office. My doctor was away and a substitute doctor gave me some packages of cream to put on the sore. It didn't help. Another year went by. The itch was spreading accross my face. This time I went to my regular doctor. She knew right away that it was skin cancer and recommended surgery. I made an appointment with the skin specialist for surgery but had to wait 3 months for a biopsy.

One day I was in a health food store and noticed a write-up about Flor.Essence. I decided to try it while I was waiting. I only took it for about 2 weeks. I quit taking it when I went on holidays. Two weeks was long enough - by the time I came home the skin cancer had totally disappeared.

This all happened about 3 years ago, now I take Flor.Essence on & off as a preventative.

F.T.

SEX female
AGE 30 years
DIAGNOSIS skin cancer
DATE

CONDITION, COMPLAINTS
itchy spot on her nose, spreading across face after a year

MEDICATION OR TREATMENT
-

HAS BEEN USING FLOR.ESSENCE SINCE
after a year and a half, while waiting for operation

RESULTS AFTER
2 weeks

CONSISTING OF
skin cancer disappeared
operation cancelled

DETAILS
still free from cancer 3 years later
still uses tea as a preventative

Cancer of the throat / stomach

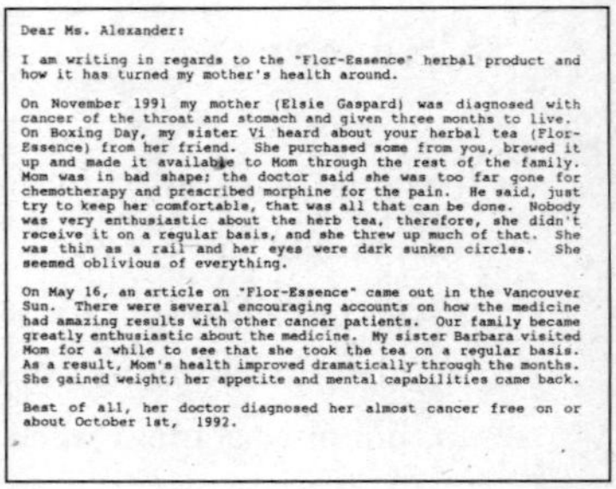

Dear Ms. Alexander:

I am writing in regards to the "Flor-Essence" herbal product and how it has turned my mother's health around.

On November 1991 my mother (Elsie Gaspard) was diagnosed with cancer of the throat and stomach and given three months to live. On Boxing Day, my sister Vi heard about your herbal tea (Flor-Essence) from her friend. She purchased some from you, brewed it up and made it available to Mom through the rest of the family. Mom was in bad shape; the doctor said she was too far gone for chemotherapy and prescribed morphine for the pain. He said, just try to keep her comfortable, that was all that can be done. Nobody was very enthusiastic about the herb tea, therefore, she didn't receive it on a regular basis, and she threw up much of that. She was thin as a rail and her eyes were dark sunken circles. She seemed oblivious of everything.

On May 16, an article on "Flor-Essence" came out in the Vancouver Sun. There were several encouraging accounts on how the medicine had amazing results with other cancer patients. Our family became greatly enthusiastic about the medicine. My sister Barbara visited Mom for a while to see that she took the tea on a regular basis. As a result, Mom's health improved dramatically through the months. She gained weight; her appetite and mental capabilities came back.

Best of all, her doctor diagnosed her almost cancer free on or about October 1st, 1992.

I am writing in regards to the 'Flor.Essence' herbal product and how it has turned my mother's health around.

On November 1991 my mother (E.G.) was diagnosed with cancer of the throat and stomach and given three months to live. On Boxing Day, my sister Vi heard about your herbal tea (Flor.Essence) from her friend. She purchased some from you, brewed it up and made it available to Mom through the rest of the family.

Mom was in bad shape; the doctor said she was too far gone for chemotherapy and prescribed morphine for the pain. He said, just try to keep her comfortable, that was all that can be done. Nobody was very enthusiastic about the herb tea, therefore, she didn't receive it on a regular basis, and she threw up much of that. She was thin as a rail and her eyes were dark sunken circles. She seemed oblivious of everything.

On May 16, an article on Flor.Essence came out in the Vancouver Sun. There were several encouraging accounts on how the medicine had amazing results with other cancer patients. Our family became greatly enthusiastic about the medicine. My sister Barbara visited Mom for a while to see that she took the tea on a regular basis. As a result, Mom's health improved dramatically through the months. She gained weight; her appetite and mental capability came back.

Best of all, her doctor diagnosed her almost cancer free on or about October 1st, 1992.

Thank you, sincerely,

W.G. Kamloops, BC Canada
november 1992

SEX female
AGE
DIAGNOSIS cancer of the throat and stomach
DATE November 1991

CONDITION, COMPLAINTS
too late for chemotherapy
weak, thin, oblivious

MEDICATION OR TREATMENT
morphine for the pain

HAS BEEN USING FLOR.ESSENCE SINCE
irregularly since December 1991
daily since May 1992

RESULTS AFTER
several months

CONSISTING OF
weight gain, improved appetite and mental capability
diagnosed almost cancer-free in October 1992

Leukemia

> This is further to your October 1995 letter to me in which you asked that I send you my testimonial regarding my son Michael.
>
> My son was diagnosed with Acute Lymphocystic Leukemia (A.L.L.) in April 1994. He was 11 years old at the time. Two weeks later I was told that because of a high chromosome count, Michael would be considered 'high risk'.
>
> Needless to say, I was in total shock -- shock and disbelief, as my son had never been sick to speak of in his whole life. I panicked. The staff of oncologists brought me into a small room to tell me about their plan of action. It would be a three year treatment plan for Michael. Phase 1 is the induction phase. Phase 2 the intensive phase and phase 3 the maintenance stage. The first two stages consisted of a lot of very strong types of chemotherapy. The last phase would be two types of chemo once a week for approximately three years!
>
> In June of 1994 I received some literature in the mail from an old friend of mine on Flor-Essence. I read the material and found it fascinating. I immediately went to the Health Food Store and bought the tea. I began Mike on 1 oz. of the tea with 2 oz. of boiled spring water both in the a.m., and p.m. His counts began to get noticeably better. The doctors' were stumped. I then made the mistake of telling them what I was giving Michael. They were not pleased with this information and basically told me not to give it to him, that it would jeopordize what they were trying to do for him. I also mentioned that I had done some research on the vitamines that he needed because of the chemo and they were completely opposed to this as well. I didn't care what they thought. I thought - they can do their thing and I will do mine!

This is further to your October 1995 letter to me in which you asked that I send you my testimonial regarding my son Michael.
My son was diagnosed with Acute Lymphocystic Leukemia (A.L.L.) in April 1994. He was 11 years old at the time. Two weeks later I was told that because of a high chromosome count, Michael would be considered 'high risk'.
Needless to say, I was in total shock - shock and disbelief, as my son had never been sick to speak of in his whole life. I panicked. The staff of oncologists brought me into a small room to tell me about their plan of action. It would be a three year treatment plan for Michael. Phase 1 is the induction phase. Phase 2 the intensive phase and phase 3 the maintenance stage. The first two stages consisted of a lot of very strong types of chemotherapy. The last phase would be two types of chemo once a week for approximately three years!
In june of 1994 I received some literature in the mail from an old friend of mine on Flor.Essence. I read the material and found it fascinating. I immediately went to the Health Food Store and bought the tea. I began Mike on 1 oz. of the tea with 2 oz. of boiled spring water both in the a.m., and p.m. His counts began to get noticeably better. The doctor's were stumped. I then made the mistake of telling them what I was giving Michael. They were not pleased with this information and basically told me not to give it to him, that it would jeopordize what they were trying to do for him. I also mentioned that I had done some research on the vitamines that he needed because of the chemo and they were completely opposed to this as well. I didn't care what they thought - they can do their thing and I will do mine!
After fase 2 of Mike's treatment, a bone-marrow aspiration was done to determine whether or not he was in remission. He was and so began the maintenance phase.

This fase of treatment entails lessor amounts of chemo over a two year period. For some reason, I didn't think Mike required the tea any longer and almost made a grave mistake because in May of 95 he suffered a relapse. The doctors tried out a new protocol on him. They were able to get him into another remission, unfortunately, it lasted only until July 17th, 1995. I tried to figure out what had happened as his counts were still so good and finally realized that the chemo was killing him without the tea to protect his organs and immune system. This was a very scary time as he also suffered a seizure (due largely to an overdose of morphine given to him in combination with .2 sodium i.v. at a rate of 0.180 instead of .9 at 0.100). Later, they told me that his heart was compromised and his liver was failing. We almost lost him and the cancer was back. Basically, I was told to take him on a holiday, he wasn't going to make it. I immediately put him back on the tea only this time I increased the dose to 2 oz. in a.m., and 2 oz. in p.m. (with appropriate amounts of water of course). I continued with the tea and vitamines on the sly - this time without the hospital knowledge. I also gave Michael echinacea which is native antibiotic and is completely natural. This regime went on for 45 days while he was in isolation. The doctors were shocked to see that his counts had come up to normal. The cancer was still there, or so they said.

In August we received the good news that they had found a unrelated donor for Mike. The doctors at his hospital told me that even if we did get Mike into remission the hospital where he was originally going to have the transplant woudn't take him. I just about hit the roof. I told him this better not be a funding thing. Anyways, I worried about this all weekend long. On the following Monday, I called over to the other hospital to find out if this were true. They said yes they would take my son even if we couldn't get him into a remission.

I took Michael over to the other hospital on September 13 th., to begin the preliminary stages for preparation of his new bone marrow. Extensive tests had to be done, e.g. heart, lungs, liver, kidneys, etc. It was noted that Michael's heart was no longer compromised nor was his liver damaged. Imagine. The transplant team were in shock and called over to his previous hospital. They couldn't seem to explain how these two organs could become completely healed! I realized then and there that the tea was responsible for this.

He was still on the tea and looking really good. On September 17 they began total body irradiation twice a day times 3 days. Each morning I gave him his tea. I also gave it to him at lunch time and before bed - a total of 6 0z. per day times 3 days. I should mention that I told the bone-marrow transplant team about the alternative medicine I was giving Mike and they encouraged me. Needless to say, instead of staying in the hospital for anywhere from 5 weeks to 3 months Mike was discharged on day 16! He broke a record. He is now at day 60 and is doing miraculously well. The tea saved my sons life. I truly believe that. Michael is still on 2 oz. in a.m. and p.m. After the 18 months to two years is up, I plan on keeping him on 1 oz. morning and night for the rest of his life. I highly recommend this tea to everyone as my son is a walking testimony for it.

I would like to take this opportunity to thank you for your encouragement throughout this very stressful time in my life and to extend special thanks to Leda for her expertise and kindness. Thanks again, from the bottom of my heart.

Sincerely, M.K. Ontario
november 1995

SEX	male
AGE	11 years
DIAGNOSIS	acute leukemia
DATE	april 1994

CONDITION, COMPLAINTS
extra risk because of high chromosome count

MEDICATION OR TREATMENT
chemotherapy for 3 years
bone marrow transplant

HAS BEEN USING FLOR.ESSENCE SINCE
June 1994

RESULTS AFTER
-

CONSISTING OF
cancer in remission

DETAILS
heart was compromised and liver damaged when use of Flor.Essence was discontinued during chemotherapy. When tea was taken again, combined with vitamins and echinacea, heart and liver fully recovered after several months. Remarkably quick recovery after bone marrow transplant.

Cancer of the liver

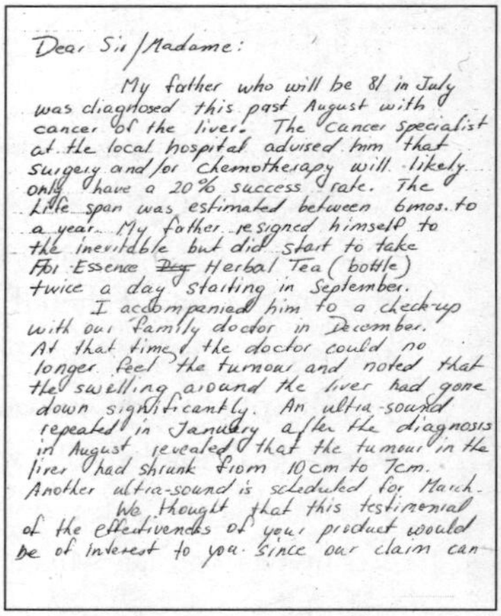
Dear Sir/Madame:
My father who will be 81 in July was diagnosed this past August with cancer of the liver. The cancer specialist at the local hospital advised him that surgery and/or chemotherapy will likely only have a 20% success rate. The life span was estimated between 6mos. to a year. My father resigned himself to the inevitable but did start to take Flor Essence ~~Dry~~ Herbal Tea (bottle) twice a day starting in September.
I accompanied him to a check-up with our family doctor in December. At that time, the doctor could no longer feel the tumour and noted that the swelling around the liver had gone down significantly. An ultra-sound repeated in January after the diagnosis in August revealed that the tumour in the liver had shrunk from 10cm to 7cm. Another ultra-sound is scheduled for March.
We thought that this testimonial of the effectiveness of your product would be of interest to you since our claim can

My father who will be 81 in July was diagnosed this past August with cancer of the liver. The cancer specialist at the local hospital advised him that surgery and/or chemotherapy will likely only have a 20% success rate. The life span was estimated between 6 months to a year. My father resigned himself to the inevitable but did start to take Flor.Essence herbal tea (bottle) twice a day starting in September.

I accompanied him to a check-up with our family doctor in December. At that time, the doctor could no longer feel the tumour and noted that the swelling around the liver had gone down significantly. An ultra-sound was repeated in January after the diagnosis in August revealed that the tumour in the liver had shrunk from 10 cm to 7 cm. Another ultrasound is scheduled for March.

We thought that this testimonial of the effectiveness of your product would be of interest to you since our claim can be proven by scientific evidence.

We have family in Germany who would like to purchase Flor.Essence over there. Do you have a distributor there or know where they could purchase your product?

Please respond at your earliest convenience.

Yours truly,

Mrs. T.M. Ontario, Canada

february 1996

SEX	male
AGE	80 years
DIAGNOSIS	cancer of the liver
DATE	August 1995

CONDITION, COMPLAINTS
only 6 months to one year left to live

MEDICATION OR TREATMENT
-

HAS BEEN USING FLOR.ESSENCE SINCE
September 1995

RESULTS AFTER
3 months

CONSISTING OF
doctor can no longer feel the tumor and notes that swelling around the liver has gone down significantly
after 4 months tumor has shrunk from 10 to 7 cm.
treatment with tea continues; next ultrasound planned a month after letter was written

Benign cancer

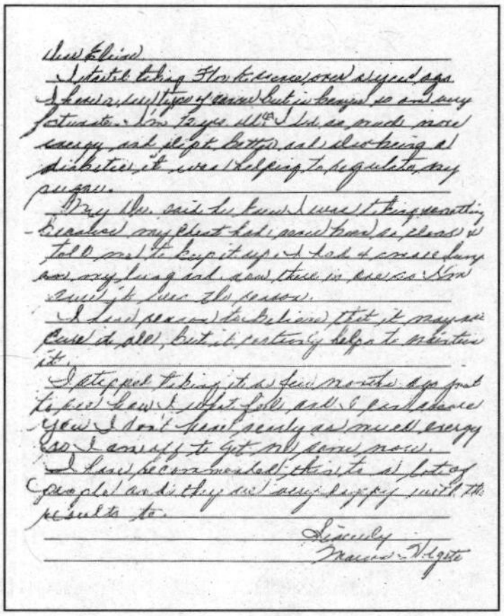
Dear Elixir,
I started taking Flor.Essence over a year ago. I have a rare type of cancer but it's benign so I am very fortunate. I'm 72 years old, female. I had so much more energy and slept better and also being a diabetic it was helping to regulate my sugar.
My doctor said he knew I was taking something because my chest had never been so clear and told me to keep it up. I had 4 small lumps on my lung and now there is one so I'm sure it was the reason.
I have reason to believe that it may not cure it all, but it certainly helps to maintain it.
I stopped taking it a few months ago just to see how I would feel and I can assure you I don't have nearly as much energy so I am off to get me some more.
I have recommended this to a lot of people and they are very happy with the results too.
Sincerely

I started taking Flor.Essence over a year ago. I have a rare type of cancer but it's benign so I am very fortunate. I'm 72 years old, female. I had so much more energy and slept better and also being a diabetic it was helping to regulate my sugar.

My doctor said he knew I was taking something because my chest had never been so clear and told me to keep it up. I had 4 small lumps on my lung and now there is one so I'm sure it was the reason.

I have reason to believe that it may not cure it all, but certainly helps to maintain it.

I stopped taking it a few months ago just to see how I would feel and I can assure you I don't have nearly as much energy so I am off to get me some more. I have recommended this to a lot of people and they are very happy with the results too.

sincerely,

M.H., British Columbia, Canada
august 1994

SEX	female
AGE	72 years
DIAGNOSIS	4 small lumps on lung
DATE	

CONDITION, COMPLAINTS
also diabetic

MEDICATION OR TREATMENT
-

HAS BEEN USING FLOR.ESSENCE SINCE
summer 1993

RESULTS AFTER
-

CONSISTING OF
3 of the 4 lumps have disappeared
more energy
improved sleep
blood sugar level easier to regulate

DETAILS
doctor notices chest has never been so clear

Chronic Fatigue Syndrome / Fybromyalgia

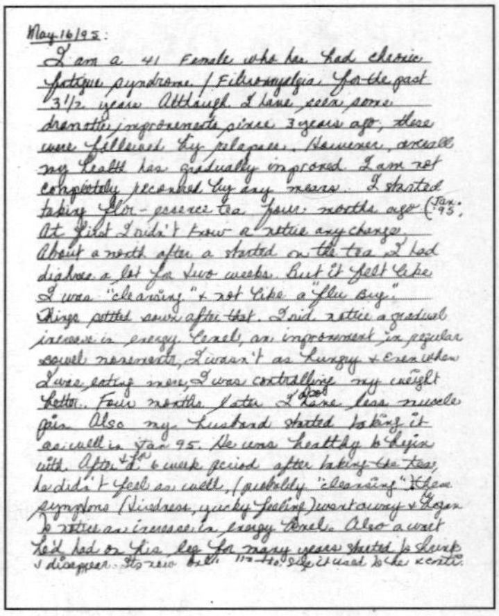
May 16/95:
I am a 41 female who has had chronic fatigue syndrome / Fibromyalgia for the past 3 1/2 years. Although I have seen some dramatic improvements since 3 years ago, these were followed by relapses. However, overall my health has gradually improved. I am not completely recovered by any means. I started taking Flor-essence tea four months ago (Jan. 95). At first I didn't know or notice any change. About a month after I started on the tea I had diarrhea a lot for two weeks. But it felt like I was "cleansing" + not like a "flu bug". Things settled down after that. I did notice a gradual increase in energy level, an improvement in regular bowel movements, I wasn't as hungry + even when I was eating more, I was controlling my weight better. Four months later I also have less muscle pain. Also my husband started taking it as well in Jan 95. He was healthy to begin with. After + for 6 week period after taking the tea, he didn't feel as well, (probably "cleansing"). These symptoms (tiredness, yucky feeling) went away + he began to notice an increase in energy level. Also a wart he'd had on his leg for many years started to shrink + disappear. Its now only 1/3 the size it used to be + conti.

I am a 41 year old female who has had Chronic Fatigue Syndrome / Fibromyalgia for the past 3,5 years. Although I have seen some dramatic improvements since 3 years ago, these were followed by relapses. However, overall my health has gradually improved. I am not completely recovered by any means. I started taking Flor.Essence tea four months ago. (Jan.95) At first I didn't know or notice any change. About a month after I started on the tea, I had diarrhea a lot for two weeks. But it felt like I was 'cleansing' and not like a 'flu bug'. Things settled down after that. I did notice a gradual increase in energy level, an improvement in regular bowel movements, I wasn't as hungry and even when I was eating more, I was controlling my weight better. Four months later I also have less muscle pain. Also my husband started taking it as well in Jan 95. He was healthy to begin with. After and for a 6 week period after taking the tea, he didn't feel as well, (probably 'cleansing'). These symptoms (tiredness, yucky feeling) went away and he began to notice an increase in energy level. Also a wart he'd had on his leg for many years started to shrink and disappear. It's now only 1/3 the size it used to be and continuing to shrink. He had tried to get rid of it before but to no avail. Also he's had eczema on his hips every winter for 10 years. This winter he did not get it at all. We are happy with the tea. Hope our testimonial helps.

K.C. Ontario, Canada, May 1995

SEX	female
AGE	41 years
DIAGNOSIS	chronic fatigue syndrome
DATE	for 3 1/2 years

CONDITION, COMPLAINTS
-

MEDICATION OR TREATMENT
-

HAS BEEN USING FLOR.ESSENCE SINCE
4 months (January 1995)

RESULTS AFTER
1 month

CONSISTING OF
diarrhea for 2 weeks
increase in energy level
improvement in regular bowel movements
controlling weight better
less muscle pain

DETAILS
partner also used Flor.Essence; a wart he'd had for many years has begun to disappear; no longer suffers from winter eczema (after 10 years of suffering from it)

Melanoma

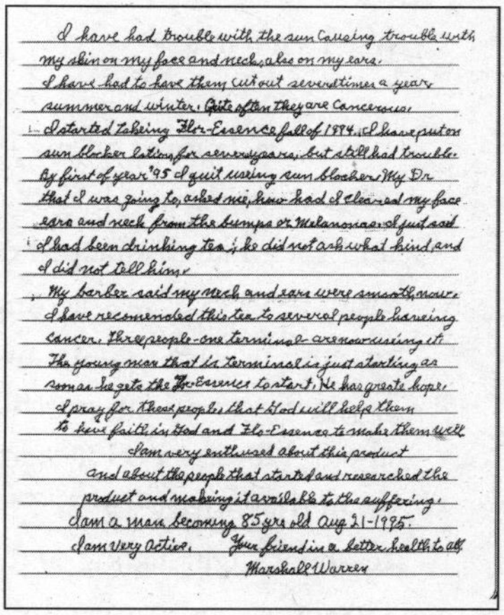
I have had trouble with the sun Causing trouble with
my skin on my face and neck, also on my ears.
I have had to have them cut out severaltimes a year,
summer and winter. Qite often they are Cancerous.
I started takeing Flor-Essence fall of 1994. I have put on
sun blocker lotion for severalyears, but still had trouble.
By first of year '95 I quit useing sun blocker. My Dr
that I was going to, asked me, how had I cleared my face
ears and neck from the bumps or Melanomias. I just said
I had been drinking tea; he did not ask what kind, and
I did not tell him.
My barber said my neck and ears were smooth now.
I have recomended this tea to several people haveing
cancer. Threepeople - one terminal - arenowusing it.
The young man that is terminal is just starting as
soon as he gets the Flo-Essence to start. He has greate hope.
I pray for these peoples that God will helps them
to have faith in God and Flo-Essence to make them well.
I am very enthused about this product
and about the people that started and researched the
product and makeing it available to the suffering.
I am a man becoming 85 yrs old Aug 21-1995.
I am very Active. Your friend in a better health to all.
Marshall Warren

I have had trouble with the sun causing trouble with my skin on my face and neck, also on my ears. I have had to have them cut out several times a year, summer and winter. Quite often they are cancerous.

I started taking Flor.Essence fall of 1994. I have put on sun blocker lotions for several years, but still had trouble. By first of year '95 I quit using sun blockers. My Dr that I was going to, asked me, how had I cleared my face, ears and neck from the bumps or melanomia. I just said I had been drinking tea, he did not ask wat kind and I did not tell him.

My barber said my neck and ears were smooth now. I have recommended this tea to several people having cancer. Three people - one terminal - are now using it. The young man that is terminal is just starting als soon as he gets the Flor.Essence to start. He has great hope.

I pray for these people that God will help them to have faith in God and Flor.Essence to make them well.

I am very enthused about this product and about the people that started and researched the product and making it available to the suffering.

I am a man becoming 85 years old aug 21-1995. I am very active.

Your friend in a better health to all.

M.W.

april 1995

SEX	male
AGE	85 years
DIAGNOSIS	melanoma on face, neck and ears
DATE	

CONDITION, COMPLAINTS
complaints continue despite using sunblock

MEDICATION OR TREATMENT
regular surgical removal, but melanoma keeps returning

HAS BEEN USING FLOR.ESSENCE SINCE
fall 1994

RESULTS AFTER
about 4 months

CONSISTING OF
face, neck and ears clear of melanoma
clear skin
increased energy

DETAILS
no longer needs sunblock

Melanoma

Name: Dorothy Cafferty
Age: 60
I had a melanoma on my left arm near elbow. This started around 1983. I was macrobiotic and I felt like this helped contain it. However around 1993 I was getting very discouraged because it wasn't going away and was getting larger in size. In my search at this time I heard about Flor Essences. I starting taking this tea around February 1993. The melanoma began to show slight fading and decreasing in size. However. one place erupted slightly around December 1993 and then disappeared with clear skin underneath. The other erupted about 2 months later in February 1994. It would bleed from time to time slightly and more tumor would then erupt. Before any eruptions it all looked the same color with no broken skin. My belief was that Flor Essence was pulling the tumor out because it began clearing around it and getting smaller and fading to a lighter color. However this second tumor kept increasing in size as it would bleed and more tumor would show immediately when this happened. It eventually projected out about 3/4 inch in height. At this time I started taking shark cartilage rectally. From February 1994 until October 1994 I used the shark cartilage as well as continuing with Flor Essence. One day I accidentally hit the tumor and it fell completely off. Of course it had been draining alot near the end and was beginning to have a whiter color. Actually it looked awful but rather harmless by this time. I certainly feel Flor Essence played a most major role in my recovery. When the tumor fell off the skin was completely clear underneath. There is still some remains of discloration on the outer edge but it continues to diminish. I'm so grateful for the product Flor Essence.

In November 1993 I had an AMAS test which indicated

I had a melanoma on my left arm near elbow. This started around 1983. I was macrobiotic and I felt like this helped contain it. However around 1993 I was getting very discouraged because it wasn't going away and was getting larger in size. In my search at this time I heard about Flor.Essence. I started taking this tea around February 1993. The melanoma began to show slight fading and decreasing in size. However, one place erupted slightly around December 1993 and then disappeared with clear skin underneath. The other erupted about 2 months later in February 1994. It would bleed from time to time slightly and more tumour would then erupt. Before any eruptions it all looked the same colour with no broken skin. My belief was that Flor.Essence was pulling the tumour out because it began clearing around it and getting smaller and fading to a lighter colour. However this second tumour kept in-creasing in size as it would bleed and more tumour would show immediately when this happened. It eventually projected about 3/4 inch in height. At this time I started out taking shark cartilage rectally. From February 1994 until October 1994 I used the shark cartilage as well as continuing with Flor.Essence. One day I accidentally hit the tumour and it fell completely off. Of course it had been draining a lot near the end and was beginning to have a whiter colour. Actually it looked awful but rather harmless by this time. I certainly feel Flor.Essence played a most major

SEX	female
AGE	60 years
DIAGNOSIS	melanoma
DATE	1983

CONDITION, COMPLAINTS
melanoma getting larger in size

MEDICATION OR TREATMENT
macrobiotic diet
from February 1994 until October 1994 used shark cartilage

HAS BEEN USING FLOR.ESSENCE SINCE
February 1993

RESULTS AFTER
-

CONSISTING OF
melanoma faded and decreased in size
November 1993 AMAS test indicated no cancer
December 1993 tumor erupted and left clear skin underneath
another tumor burst 2 months later, but continued to bleed occasionally and grew to 3/4 inch in height
late 1994 this tumor too fell off (looking whiter but harmless by this time)

DETAILS
skin underneath tumor was clear

role in my recovery. When the tumour fell off the skin was completely clear underneath. There is still some remains of discoloration on the outer edge but it continues to diminish. I'm so grateful for the product Flor.Essence. In November 1993 I had an AMAS test which indicated no cancer in my body. This was prior to the tumours erupting. Also I never had a biopsy taken because I was fearful of the melanoma spreading. Every doctor that looked at it thought it was melanoma and it was diagnosed in Mexico as a melanoma.

D.C., Arizona, USA
november 1995

Multiple sclerose (M.S.)

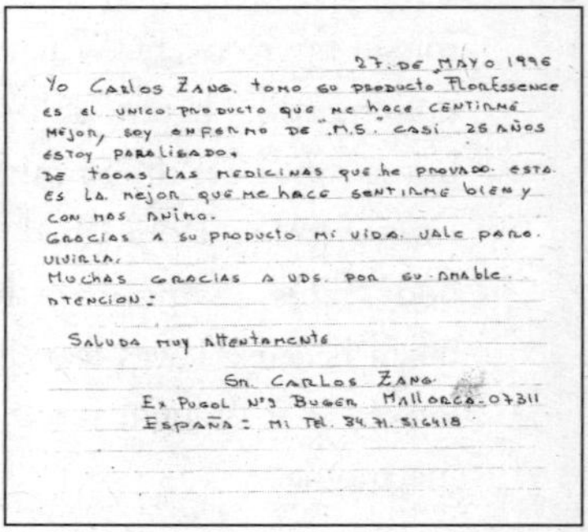

27. DE MAYO 1996
Yo Carlos Zang. tomo su producto Flor.Essence
es el unico producto que me hace centirme
mejor, soy enfermo de ".M.S." casi 25 años
estoy paralisado.
De todas las medicinas que he provado esta
es la mejor que me hace sentirme bien y
con mas animo.
Gracias a su producto mi vida vale para
vivirla.
Muchas gracias a uds. por su amable
atencion:

Saluda muy attentamente

Sr. Carlos Zang
Ex Pugol Nº3 Buger Mallorca-07311
España: mi Tel. 34.71.516418

Yo Carlos Zang. Tomo su producto Flor.Essence es el unico producto que me hace centirme mejor, soy enferno de 'M.S.' casi zsanos estoy paralisado.
De todas las medicinas que he provado esta es la mejor que me hace sentirme bien y con mas animo.
Gracias a su producto mi vida vale para vivirla. Muchas gracias a uds. por su amable atencion.
Saluda muy attentamente.

My name is Carlos Zang. I use your product Flor.Essence. It's the only product that makes me feel better. I have been ill with M.S. for almost 25 years. I am paralyzed. Of all the medication I have tried, this is the best: it makes me feel better and it lifts my spirit.
Thanks to your product my life is worth living again. Many thanks for your kind attention.

Sincerely, C.Z.

SEX	male
AGE	
DIAGNOSIS	multiple sclerosis
DATE	for 25 years

CONDITION, COMPLAINTS
paralyzed

MEDICATION OR TREATMENT
tried everything

HAS BEEN USING FLOR.ESSENCE SINCE
-

RESULTS AFTER
-

CONSISTING OF
feeling of well-being and courage

DETAILS
testimonial written by a friend and signed with a fingerprint

Multiple sclerose (M.S.)

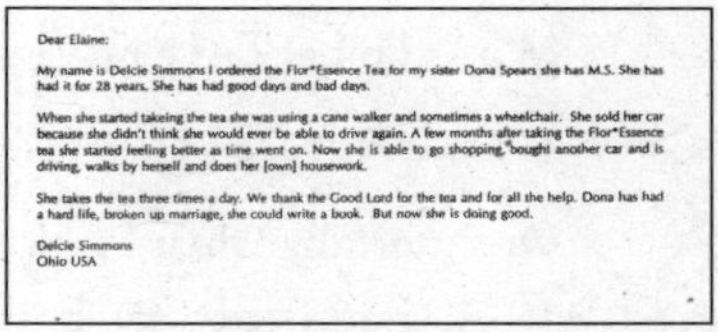
Dear Elaine:

My name is Delcie Simmons I ordered the Flor*Essence Tea for my sister Dona Spears she has M.S. She has had it for 28 years. She has had good days and bad days.

When she started takeing the tea she was using a cane walker and sometimes a wheelchair. She sold her car because she didn't think she would ever be able to drive again. A few months after taking the Flor*Essence tea she started feeling better as time went on. Now she is able to go shopping, bought another car and is driving, walks by herself and does her [own] housework.

She takes the tea three times a day. We thank the Good Lord for the tea and for all the help. Dona has had a hard life, broken up marriage, she could write a book. But now she is doing good.

Delcie Simmons
Ohio USA

My name is D.S. I ordered the Flor.Essence Tea for my sister D.S. she has Multiple Sclerose. She has had it for 28 years. She has had good days and bad days.

When she started taking the tea she was using a cane walker and sometimes a wheelchair. She sold her car because she didn't think she would ever be able to drive again. A few months after taking the Flor.Essence tea she started feeling better as time went on. Now she is able to go shopping, bought another car and is driving, walks by herself and does her (own) housework. She takes the tea three times a day. We thank the Good Lord for the tea and for all the help. D. has had a hard life, broken up marriage, she could write a book. But now she is doing good.

D.S. Ohio USA

SEX	female
AGE	
DIAGNOSIS	multiple sclerosis
DATE	for 28 years

CONDITION, COMPLAINTS
uses walking cane, sometimes a wheelchair
unable to drive a car

MEDICATION OR TREATMENT
-

HAS BEEN USING FLOR.ESSENCE SINCE
several months

RESULTS AFTER
several months

CONSISTING OF
feeling better and better
can shop, drive, and walk again and does own housework

DETAILS
tea taken three times a day

Multiple sclerose (M.S.)

One morning when I woke up in the spring of 1974, I realized that both of my legs were quite heavy and that I could no longer move them. Gradually after a week's time, I was able to move them slightly. I was hospitalized for a few weeks. When I finally got out, I had to walk with a cane for many months. In the fall of 1980 I began having blood pressure problems which I was able to control with the help of medication. Following surgery for the removal of a slipped disc in the spring of 1986, problems with my equilibrum, with dizziness, with unexplained fatigue and with my vision appeared. I began having bladder control problems in the beginning of 1987 and in the summer, I became paralysed once again but only on the left side. From 1987 to 1992 I paralysed several times. Doctors had diagnozed me as having multiple sclerosis, neurogenic bladder, essential labile blood pressure. I lived from bed to wheelchair, never leaving my cane behind. Only in 1990 was I hospitalized for 154 days, following that incident I had to resign myself to quitting my job. I don't have to mention that mentally I was not doing too well. I was being treated by neurologists, urologists, nephrologists, psychiatrists, physiotherapists and occupational therapists. I took a lot of medication: many of which were steroid and cortisone treatments. I wore a prothesis on my left foot for over one year.

At the end of November 1992, I had heard of Flor.Essence and it was only at the end of January 1993 that I began my treatment. In the beginning I took 3 doses of 56 ml daily which was reduced after two weeks to 2 doses of 56 ml per day. During that same period I followed a rehabilitation program that was offered by a rehabilitation center in my area. After 4 weeks I began to notice that my fatigue had substantially decreased and nonetheless, I found some hidden strenghts that had been previously lost.

One morning, when I woke up in the spring of 1974, I realized that both of my legs were quite heavy and that I could no longer move them. Gradually after a week's time, I was able to move them slightly. I was hospitalized for a few weeks. When I finally got out, I had to walk with a cane for many months. In the fall of 1980 I began having blood pressure problems which I was able to control with the help of medication. Following surgery for the removal of a slipped disc in the spring of 1986, problems with my equilibrium, with dizziness, with unexplained fatigue and with my vision appeared. I began having bladder control problems in the beginning of 1987 and in the summer, I became paralyzed once again but only on the left side.

From 1987 to 1992 I paralyzed seven times. Doctors had diagnosed me as having MULTIPLE SCLEROSIS, NEUROGENIC BLADDER, ESSENTIAL LABILE BLOOD PRESSURE. I lived from my bed to my wheelchair, never leaving my cane behind. Only in 1990 was I hospitalized for 154 days, following that incident I had to resign myself to quitting my job. I don't have to mention that mentally I was not doing too well. I was being treated by neurologists, urologists, nephrologists, psychiatrists, physiotherapists and occupational therapists. I took a lot of medication: many of which were steroid and cortisone treatments. I wore a prothesis on my left foot for over one year.

At the end of November 1992, I had heard of Flor.Essence and it was only at the end of January 1993 that I began my treatment. In the beginning I took 3 doses of 56 ml daily which was reduced after two weeks to 2 doses of 56 ml per day. During that same period I followed a rehabilitation program that was offered by a rehabilitation center in my area. After 4 weeks I began to notice that my fatigue had substantially decreased and nonetheless, I found some hidden strengths that had been previously lost.

For the very first time at the end of April 1993, I walked without a cane. I was physically evaluated at the time I had started my rehabilitation program and when I completed the program at the end of May 1993, I had improved by more than 200%.

On this day, August 1st, 1993, I walk without a cane, I no longer take any medication, my physical state is almost back to normal and the problems with my equilibrium, my dizziness, my vision, my fatigue and my bladder have all disappeared. My mental state is quite good. At the age of 42 with a Multiple Sclerosis label, I thank God that I am aware of Flor.Essence, a magic potion that convinces me that my quality of life can improve.

Gilles Rioux

For the very first time at the end of April 1993, I walked without a cane. I was physically evaluated at the time I had started my rehabilitation program and when I completed the program at the end of May 1993, I had improved by more than 200%.

On this day, August 1st 1993, I walk without a cane, I no longer take any medication, my physical state is almost back to normal and the problems with my equilibrum, my dizziness, my vision, my fatigue and my bladder have all disappeared. My mental state is quite good. At the age of 42 with a Multiple Sclerose label, I thank God that I am aware of Flor.Essence, a magic potion that convinces me that quality of life can improve.

G.R.
August 1993

SEX	male
AGE	42
DIAGNOSIS	multiple sclerosis
DATE	1987

CONDITION, COMPLAINTS
equilibrium problems, dizziness, fatigue, impaired vision, loss of bladder control, paralysis
lived between bed and wheelchair

MEDICATION OR TREATMENT
treated by various specialists
lots of medication including steroid and cortisone treatments

HAS BEEN USING FLOR.ESSENCE SINCE
January 1993

RESULTS AFTER
4 weeks

CONSISTING OF
less fatigue
after 3 months walked without a cane
after 4 months, improved 'by more than 200%'
after 7 months, no complaints, physical condition almost back to normal, no longer takes medication

Cancer of the pancreas

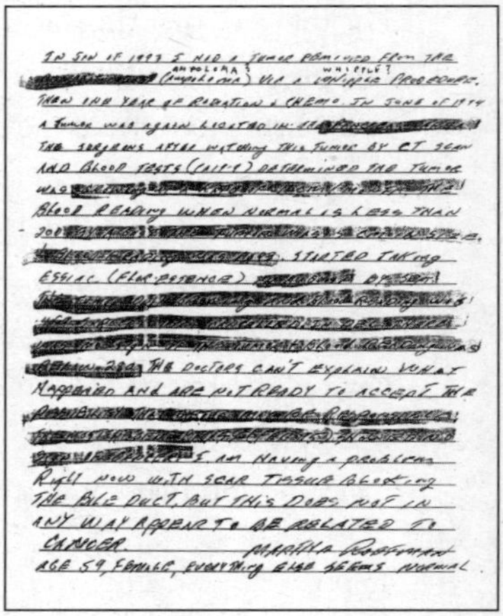
IN JAN OF 1993 I HAD A TUMOR REMOVED FROM THE
AMPOLOMA? WHIPPLE?
[redacted] (ampoloma) VIA A WHIPPLE PROCEDURE.
THEN ONE YEAR OF RADIATION & CHEMO. IN JUNE OF 1994
A TUMOR WAS AGAIN LOCATED IN [redacted]
THE SURGEONS AFTER WATCHING THIS TUMOR BY CT SCAN
AND BLOOD TESTS (LA19-9) DETERMINED THE TUMOR
WAS [redacted]
BLOOD READING WHEN NORMAL IS LESS THAN
200 [redacted]. STARTED TAKING
ESSIAC (FLOR-ESSENCE) [redacted]
THE DOCTORS CAN'T EXPLAIN WHAT
HAPPENED AND ARE NOT READY TO ACCEPT THE
[redacted] I AM HAVING A PROBLEM
RIGHT NOW WITH SCAR TISSUE BLOCKING
THE BILE DUCT, BUT THIS DOES NOT IN
ANY WAY APPEAR TO BE RELATED TO
CANCER. [illegible]
AGE 59, FEMALE, EVERYTHING ELSE SEEMS NORMAL

In jan of 1993 I had a tumor removed from the pancreatic duct (ampoloma) via a whipple procedure. Then one year of radiation & chemo. In june of 1994 a tumor was again located in the pancreas area. The surgeons after watching this tumor by CT scan and blood tests (LA19-9) determined the tumor was growing at a rate of 1 cm/month. The blood reading when normal is less than 200. By august the tumor was 5 cm in size / blood reading was 1093. Started taking Essiac (Flor.Essence) in august by sept.
The tumor quit growing and blood reading was 459. Surgery was cancelled. In dec there was no sign of the tumor + blood reading was below 280. The doctor's can't explain what happened and are not ready to accept the possibility that the tea may be responsible: the most recent biopsy (feb 95) showed no sign of cancer.
I am having a problem right now with scar tissue blocking the bile duct, but this does not in any way appear to be related to cancer.
Age 59, female, everything else seems normal.

M.R., Texas
februari 1995

SEX	female
AGE	59
DIAGNOSIS	cancer of the pancreas
DATE	June 1994

CONDITION, COMPLAINTS
previous tumor had been removed
new tumor grew 1 centimeter a month

MEDICATION OR TREATMENT
1 year of chemotherapy and radiotherapy
due to be operated

HAS BEEN USING FLOR.ESSENCE SINCE
August 1994

RESULTS AFTER
several weeks

CONSISTING OF
tumor growth stopped
after 4 months no trace of tumor
after 6 months, biopsy showed no sign of cancer

DETAILS
scar tissue blocking bile duct
operation cancelled

Bell's palsy

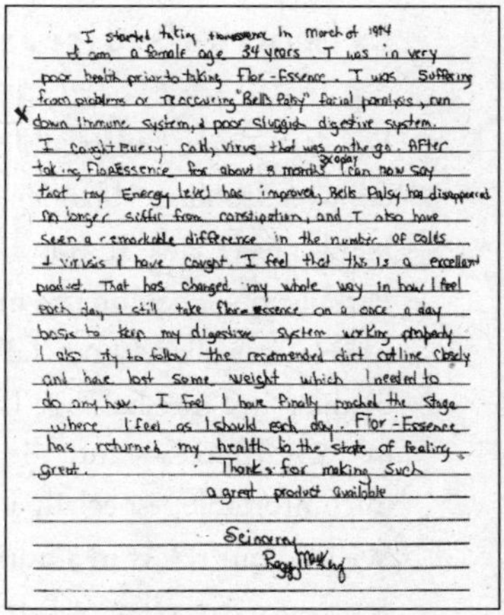

I started taking ~~[illegible]~~ in march of 1994
I am a female age 34 years. I was in very
poor health prior to taking Flor-Essence. I was suffering
from problems or reoccuring "Bells Palsy" facial paralysis, run
down immune system, a poor sluggish digestive system.
I caught every cold, virus that was on the go. After
taking FlorEssence for about 3 months 3x a day I can now say
that my Energy level has improved, Bells Palsy has disappeared
no longer suffer from constipation, and I also have
seen a remarkable difference in the number of colds
& virusis I have caught. I feel that this is a excellent
product. That has changed my whole way in how I feel
each day, I still take flor-essence on a once a day
basis to keep my digestive system working properly
I also try to follow the recommended diet outline closely
and have lost some weight which I needed to
do any how. I feel I have finally reached the stage
where I feel as I should each day. Flor-Essence
has returned my health to the state of feeling
great. Thanks for making such
a great product available

Seincerey
Peggy McKay

I started taking Flor.Essence in March of 1994. I am a female age 34 years. I was in very poor health prior to taking Flor.Essence. I was suffering from problems or reoccurring 'Bell's Palsy' facial paralysis, run down immune system, a poor sluggish digestive system.

I caught every cold, virus that was on the go. After taking Flor.Essence for about 3 months 3x a day I can now say that my energy level has improved, Bells Palsy has disappeared, no longer suffer from constipation, and I also have seen remarkable difference in the number of colds & virusis I have cought. I feel that this is a excellent product. That has changed my whole way in how I feel.

Each day I still take Flor.Essence on a once a day basis to keep my digestive system working properly. I also try to follow the recommended diet outline closely and have lost some weight which I needed to do anyhow. I feel I have finally reached the stage where I feel as I should each day. Flor.Essence has returned my health to the state of feeling great.

Thanks for making such a great product available.

P. Mc K.

SEX female
AGE 34
DIAGNOSIS Bell's palsy
DATE

CONDITION, COMPLAINTS
facial paralysis
run-down immune system
sluggish digestive system

MEDICATION OR TREATMENT
diet

HAS BEEN USING FLOR.ESSENCE SINCE
3 months

RESULTS AFTER
3 months

CONSISTING OF
more energy
no more Bell's palsy
no longer constipated
less colds and virus infections
some weight loss (which had been needed)
feels great

Parkinson's disease

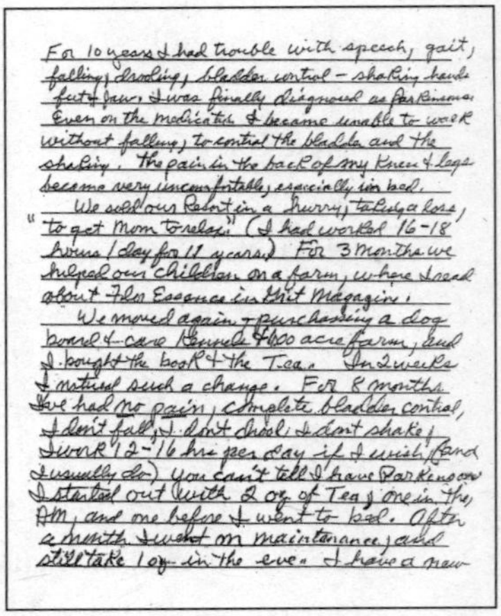
For 10 years I had trouble with speech, gait, falling, drooling, bladder control - shaking hands feet & jaw. I was finally diagnosed as Parkinsons. Even on the medication I became unable to walk without falling, to control the bladder and the shaking. The pain in the back of my knees & legs became very uncomfortable, especially in bed.
We sold our Resort in a hurry, taking a loss, "to get Mom to relax." (I had worked 16-18 hours/day for 11 years.) For 3 months we helped our children on a farm, where I read about Flor Essence in Grit Magazine.
We moved again - purchasing a dog board & care kennels & 1000 acre farm, and I bought the book & the Tea. In 2 weeks I noticed such a change. For 8 months I've had no pain, complete bladder control, I don't fall, I don't drool; I don't shake; I work 12-16 hrs per day if I wish (and I usually do) You can't tell I have Parkinsons. I started out with 2 oz of Tea; one in the AM, and one before I went to bed. After a month I went on maintenance, and still take 1 oz in the eve. I have a new

For 10 years I had trouble with speech, gait, falling, drooling, bladder control - shaking hands, feet, jaw. It was finally diagnosed as Parkinson's. Even on the medication I became unable to walk without falling, to control the bladder and the shaking. The pain in the back of my knees and legs became very uncomfortable, especially in bed.

We sold our resort in a hurry, taking a loss, 'to get Mom to relax'. (I have worked 16-18 hours/day for 11 years) For 3 months we helped our children on a farm, where I read about Flor.Essence in Grit Magazine.

We moved again - purchasing a dog board and care kennel and 1000 acre farm, and I bought the book and the tea. In two weeks I noticed such a change. For 8 months I've had no pain, complete bladder control, I don't fall, I don't drool, I don't shake, I work 12-16 hours per day if I wish (and I usually do). You can't tell I have Parkinson's. I started out with 2 oz of tea, one in the am and one before I went to bed. After a month I went on maintenance, and I still take 1 oz in the eve. I have a new lease on life.

R.D.
Minnesota, USA

SEX	female
AGE	65 years
DIAGNOSIS	Parkinson's disease
DATE	for 10 years

CONDITION, COMPLAINTS
trouble speaking, walking, controlling bladder
shaking hands, feet, jaw
pain in knees and legs

MEDICATION OR TREATMENT

HAS BEEN USING FLOR.ESSENCE SINCE
-

RESULTS AFTER
2 weeks

CONSISTING OF
complaints disappeared
no more signs of Parkinson
back at original high level of energy

DETAILS
'I have a new lease on life.'

Pre-cancerous spots on the skin

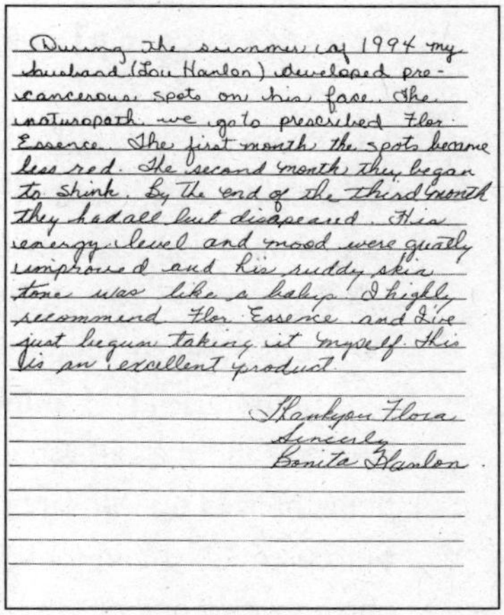
During the summer of 1994 my husband (Lou Hanlon) developed pre-cancerous spots on his face. The naturopath we go to prescribed Flor. Essence. The first month the spots become less red. The second month they began to shink. By the end of the third month they had all but disapeared. His energy level and mood were greatly improved and his ruddy skin tone was like a baby's. I highly recommend Flor. Essence and I've just begun taking it myself. this is an excellent product.

Thankyou Flora
Sincerly
Bonita Hanlon.

During the summer of 1994 my husband (L. H.) developed pre-cancerous spots on his face. The naturopath we go to prescribed Flor.Essence. The first month the spots became less red. The second month they began to shrink. By the end of the third month they had all but disappeared. His energy level and mood were greatly improved and his ruddy skin tone was like a baby's. I highly recom-mend Flor.Essence and I've just begun taking it myself. This is an excellent product. Thank you, Flora.

Sincerely,
B.N., Saskatchewan, Canada april 1996

SEX	male
AGE	
DIAGNOSIS	pre-cancerous spots on the face
DATE	summer 1994

CONDITION, COMPLAINTS
-

MEDICATION OR TREATMENT
-

HAS BEEN USING FLOR.ESSENCE SINCE
summer 1994

RESULTS AFTER
1 month

CONSISTING OF
spots became less red
the second month spots began to disappear
after three months they had all but disappeared

DETAILS
greatly improved energy level and mood

Prostate complaints

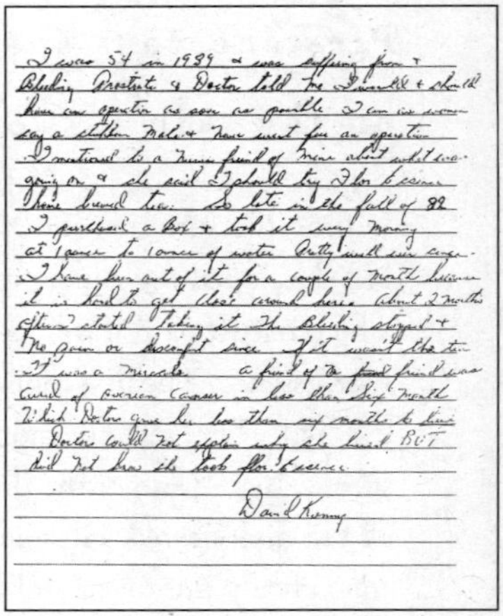

I was 54 in 1989 & was suffering from a
Bleeding Prostate & Doctor told me I would & should
have an operation as soon as possible I am as women
say a stubborn Male & never went for an operation
I mentioned to a nurse friend of mine about what was
going on & she said I should try Flor Essence
home brewed tea. So late in the fall of 92
I purchased a box & took it every morning
at 1 ounce to 1 ounce of water Pretty well since.
I have been out of it for a couple of month because
it is hard to get close around here. About 2 months
after I started taking it the Bleeding stopped &
no pain or discomfort since. If it wasn't the tea
it was a miracle. a friend of my friend was
cured of ovarian cancer in less than six month
which Doctors gave her less than six months to live
Doctors could not explain why she lived BUT
did not know she took flor Essence

David Kenny

I was 54 in 1989 and was suffering from a bleeding prostate and doctor told me I would and should have an operation as soon as possible. I am as women say a 'stubborn male' and never went for an operation. I mentioned to a nurse friend of mine about what was going on and she said I should try Flor.Essence home brewed tea. So, late in the fall of 1992 I purchased a box and took it every morning at one ounce to one ounce of water. Pretty well ever since. I have been out of it for a couple of months because it is hard to get close around here. About 2 months after I started taking it the bleeding stopped and no pain or discomfort since. If it wasn't the tea it was a miracle. A friend was cured of ovarian cancer in less than six months. Doctors gave her less than six months to live. Doctors could not explain why she lived BUT did not know she took Flor.Essence.

D.K.
Manitoba, CANADA

SEX	male
AGE	54 years
DIAGNOSIS	bleeding prostate
DATE	1989

CONDITION, COMPLAINTS
bleeding prostate, pain
to be operated on as soon as possible

MEDICATION OR TREATMENT
-

HAS BEEN USING FLOR.ESSENCE SINCE
fall 1992

RESULTS AFTER
2 months

CONSISTING OF
bleeding stopped
no more pain or discomfort

DETAILS
friend took Flor.Essence and was cured of ovarian cancer in less than 6 months, although doctors had given her less than six months to live

Prostate cancer / lymph cancer

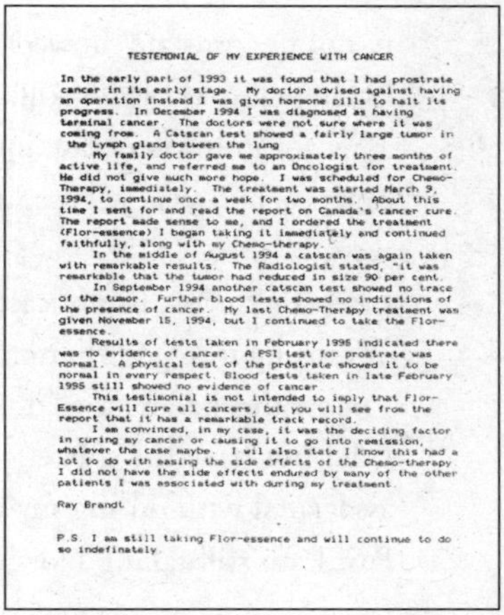
TESTEMONIAL OF MY EXPERIENCE WITH CANCER

In the early part of 1993 it was found that I had prostrate cancer in its early stage. My doctor advised against having an operation instead I was given hormone pills to halt its progress. In December 1994 I was diagnosed as having terminal cancer. The doctors were not sure where it was coming from. A Catscan test showed a fairly large tumor in the Lymph gland between the lung

My family doctor gave me approximately three months of active life, and referred me to an Oncologist for treatment. He did not give much more hope. I was scheduled for Chemo-Therapy, immediately. The treatment was started March 9, 1994, to continue once a week for two months. About this time I sent for and read the report on Canada's cancer cure. The report made sense to me, and I ordered the treatment (Flor-essence) I began taking it immediately and continued faithfully, along with my Chemo-therapy.

In the middle of August 1994 a catscan was again taken with remarkable results. The Radiologist stated, "it was remarkable that the tumor had reduced in size 90 per cent.

In September 1994 another catscan test showed no trace of the tumor. Further blood tests showed no indications of the presence of cancer. My last Chemo-Therapy treatment was given November 15, 1994, but I continued to take the Flor-essence.

Results of tests taken in February 1995 indicated there was no evidence of cancer. A PSI test for prostrate was normal. A physical test of the prostrate showed it to be normal in every respect. Blood tests taken in late February 1995 still showed no evidence of cancer

This testimonial is not intended to imply that Flor-Essence will cure all cancers, but you will see from the report that it has a remarkable track record.

I am convinced, in my case, it was the deciding factor in curing my cancer or causing it to go into remission, whatever the case maybe. I wil also state I know this had a lot to do with easing the side effects of the Chemo-therapy I did not have the side effects endured by many of the other patients I was associated with during my treatment.

Ray Brandt

P.S. I am still taking Flor-essence and will continue to do so indefinately.

In the early part of 1993 it was found that I had prostate cancer in its early stage. My doctor advised against having an operation. Instead I was given hormone pills to halt its progress. In December 1994 I was diagnosed as having terminal cancer. The doctors were not sure where it was coming from. A CAT scan test showed a faily large tumour in the Lymph gland between the lung.

My family doctor gave me approximately three months of active life, and referred me to an Oncologist for treatment. Het did not give much more hope. I was scheduled for chemotherapy immediately. The treatment was started March 9, 1994, to continue once a week for two months. About this time I sent for and read the report on Canada's cancer cure. The report made sense to me, and I ordered the treatment (Flor.Essence). I began taking it immediately and continued faithfully, along with my chemotherapy.

SEX	male
AGE	
DIAGNOSIS/	prostate cancer (early 1993)
DATE	lymph cancer (December 1994)

CONDITION, COMPLAINTS
terminal, 3 months left to live

MEDICATION OR TREATMENT
chemotherapy March-November 1994

HAS BEEN USING FLOR.ESSENCE SINCE
March 1994

RESULTS AFTER
5 months

CONSISTING OF
eased chemotherapy side effects
tumor reduced in size by 90%
after 6 months, tumor had gone, free from cancer

In the middel of August 1994 a CAT scan was again taken with remarkable results. The Radiologist state, 'it was remarkable that the tumour had reduced in size 90 per cent.'

In September 1994 another CAT scan test showed no trace of the tumour. Further blood tests showed no indications of the presence of cancer. My last chemotherapy treatment was given November 15, 1994, but I continued to take the Flor.Essence.

Results of tests taken in February 1995 indicated that there was no evidence of cancer. A PSA test for prostate was normal. A physical

test of the prostate showed it to be normal in every respect. Blood tests taken in late February 1994 still showed no evidence of cancer.
This testimonial is not intended to imply that Flor.Essence will cure all cancers, but you will see from the report that it has a remarkable track record.
I am convinced, in my case, it was the deciding factor in curing my cancer or causing it to go into remission. Whatever the case may be. I will also state I know this had a lot to do with easing the side effects of the chemotherapy. I did not have the side effects endured by many of the other patients I was associated with during my treatment.
P.S. I am still taking Flor.Essence and will continue to do so indefinitely.

R.B. Arizona, USA
december 1995

Prostate cancer

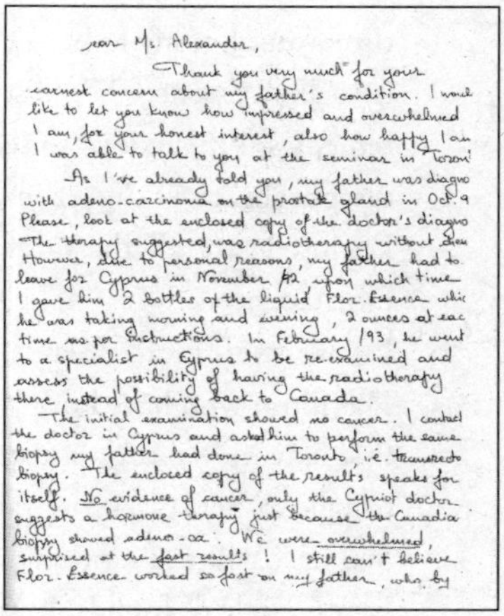
Dear Ms. Alexander,
Thank you very much for your earnest concern about my father's condition. I would like to let you know how impressed and overwhelmed I am, for your honest interest, also how happy I am I was able to talk to you at the seminar in Toronto!
As I've already told you, my father was diagno with adeno-carcinoma on the prostate gland in Oct. 9 Please, look at the enclosed copy of the doctor's diagno The therapy suggested, was radiotherapy without chem However, due to personal reasons, my father had to leave for Cyprus in November 92 upon which time I gave him 2 bottles of the liquid Flor. Essence whic he was taking morning and evening, 2 ounces at eac time as per instructions. In February /93, he went to a specialist in Cyprus to be re-examined and assess the possibility of having the radiotherapy there instead of coming back to Canada.
The initial examination showed no cancer. I contact the doctor in Cyprus and asked him to perform the same biopsy my father had done in Toronto, i.e. transrecto biopsy. The enclosed copy of the result's speaks for itself. No evidence of cancer, only the Cypriot doctor suggests a hormone therapy just because the Canadia biopsy showed adeno-ca. We were overwhelmed, surprised at the fast results! I still can't believe Flor. Essence worked so fast on my father, who, by

Thank you very much for your earnest concern about my father's condition. I would like to let you know how impressed and overwhelmed I am, for your honest interest, also how happy I am I was able to talk to you at the seminar in Toronto.

As I've already told you, my father was diagnosed with adeno-carcinoma on the prostate gland in Oct. 1992. Please, look at the enclosed copy of the doctor's diagnose. The therapy suggested, was radiotherapy without chemo. However, due to personal rea-sons, my father had to leave for Cyprus in November 1992, upon which time I gave him 2 bottles of the liquid Flor.Essence which he was taking morning and evening, 2 ounces at each time per instructions. In February 1993 he went to a specialist in Cyprus to be re-examined and assess the possibility of having the radiotherapy there, instead of coming back to Canada.

The initial examination showed no cancer. I contacted the doctor in Cyprus and asked him to perform the same biopsy my father had done in Toronto, i.e. transrectal biopsy. The enclosed copy of the results speaks for itself. No evidence of cancer, only the Cypriot doctor suggests a hormone therapy just because the Canadian biopsy showed adeno-carcinoma. We were overwhelmed, surprised at the fast results! I still can't believe Flor.Essence worked so fast on my father, who, by the way, is not a very good keeper of diet or health regiments. He consumes a lot of sugar (which is as you said to me in Toronto, an enemy for cancer patients!)

I sent him more supplies of Flor.Essence and told him to continue taking it, but my real triumph will be, when I can convince him to come back to Toronto to be checked again by the same doctor who originally found the cancer!

I have an appointment to talk to my doctor and tell him about the turnaround of my father's condition but I really don't think he will attribute it to Flor.Essence. We discussed it before and he doesn't believe in herbal remedies. I'm anxious to see, though, how he is going to explain the sudden disappearance of cancer in 2 months.

Enclosed, are all the facts of my father's condition, before and after the Flor.Essence.

I have two more friends, one in Windsor, Ontario, the other one in Hamilton who have both lymphatic cancer and are taking Flor.Essence. The first lady in Windsor is also under experimental treatment. If you would like to talk to her, please let me know, I will give you her name and phoneno. She needs all the support and encouragement!

In our circle of friends, I was perhaps the first one to know about Essiac back in 1977, from Homemakers magazine. I'm so sad that the government has not even allowed it as mercy remedy for those who have no other hope! They have other drugs which are supplied on mercy grounds for Aids and other incurable diseases!

Do you think that Flor.Essence will be ever allowed to prove its miraculous effect on cancer patients? How can we, the people who Flor.Essence, help to make it known to those who need it?

Please, acknowledge receipt of my letter. Promising to keep in touch.

Regards, E.E.
May 1993

SEX male
AGE
DIAGNOSIS adeno-carcinoma on the prostate gland
DATE October 1992

CONDITION, COMPLAINTS
-

MEDICATION OR TREATMENT
recommended radiotherapy was not performed for private reasons

HAS BEEN USING FLOR.ESSENCE SINCE
November 1992

RESULTS AFTER
3 months

CONSISTING OF
free from cancer

DETAILS
copies of doctors' diagnoses had been enclosed

Brain tumor / spinal tumor

I wanted to tell you our experience with Flor.Essence. In June of 1994, our 8 year old daughter, Amy, was diagnosed with a rare form of brain cancer. It's called ependymoma. Along with tumor on her brain stem, it had metastasized (spread) throughout her spinal cord. After performing a 5 1/2 hour surgery on her brain stem - to remove what they safely could, we were told that our daughter had 3 month to maybe a year at the most, to live. We began chemotherapy - but it didn't work. She received radiation treatments - 2 treatments a day, for seven weeks. Amy looked awful - then on March 28, 1995 we started the Flor.Essence tea. I followed Elaine Alexander's orders regarding the proper diet, consistency with tea, and lots of bottled water - to properly cleanse the body. Gradually we saw improvements....

Every 3 to 4 months an MRI of Amy's brain and spine showed slight sprinkage. We constantly told Amy to think positively and to imagine the radiation and tea eating her cancer like PacMan. We also did visual-imagery to control pain and reflexology to relax her body. As time went on, Amy began to gain weight and feel stronger.

The great news came on June 13th, 1996 - Amy's brain tumor is gone!! The mass is not appearing on the MRI - which is incredible! - and the tumors in her spine are shrinking. We're still concerned about Amy's spine, but this is an incredible mile stone.

I wanted to tell you our experience with Flor*Essence. In June of 1994, our 8 year old daughter, Amy, was diagnosed with a rare form of brain cancer. It's called ependymoma. Along with tumour on her brain stem, it had metastasized (spread) throughout her spinal cord. After performing a 5 1/2 hour surgery on her brain stem - to remove what they safely could, we were told that our daughter had 3 months to maybe a year at the most, to live. We began chemotherapy - but it didn't work. The she received radiation treatments - 2 treatments a day, for seven weeks. Amy looked awful - then on March 28, 1995 we started the Flor*Essence tea. I followed Elaine Alexander's orders regarding the proper diet, consistency with tea, and lots of bottled water - to properly cleanse the body. Gradually we saw improvements...

Every 3 to 4 months an MRI of Amy's brain and spine showed slight shrinkage. We constantly told Amy to think positively and to imagine the radiation and tea eating her cancer like PacMan. We also did visual-imagery to control pain and reflexology to relax her body. As time went on, Amy began to gain weight and feel stronger.

The great news came on June 13th, 1996 - Amy's brain tumour is gone!! The mass is not appearing on the MRI - which is incredible! - and the tumours in her spine are shrinking. We're still concerned about Amy's spine, but this is an incredible mile stone.

Everyone is amazed at how good Amy's doing!!

I would tell anyone that has cancer, to begin taking Flor*Essence immediately. After several weeks on the tea I noticed an improvement in my daughter's immune system and energy level. I'm not quite sure if the radiation stopped my daughter's tumour from growing - and then the tea efficated the tumour or if the tea played a much larger role. I do know the tea is very much an important part, with my daughter's progress.

I will continue to write to you Leda, and update you on Amy's progress.

Thanks for all you do

Regards,

Sue Lyon

SEX	female
AGE	8 years
DIAGNOSIS	ependymoma (tumor in brain and spinal cord)
DATE	June 1994

CONDITION, COMPLAINTS
tumor in brain, metastasized throughout spinal cord
3 months to one year left to live

MEDICATION OR TREATMENT
part of brain tumor surgically removed
chemotherapy didn't work
radiotherapy for 7 weeks

HAS BEEN USING FLOR.ESSENCE SINCE
March 1995, in combination with diet and lots of bottled water

RESULTS AFTER
several months

CONSISTING OF
tumor decreased in size
weight gain
more energy
on June 13, 1996, brain tumor had disappeared completely, tumors in spine are shrinking

DETAILS
it is not clear if improvement resulted from the use of Flor.Essence or from radiotherapy

Everyone is amazed at how good Amy's doing!!
I would tell anyone that has cancer, to begin taking Flor.Essence immediately. After several weeks on the tea I noticed an improvement in my daughter's immune system and energy level. I'm not quite sure if the radiation stopped my daughter's tumor from growing - and then the tea afficated the tumor or if the tea played a much larger role. I do know the tea is very much an important part, with my daughter's progress.
I will continue to write to you Leda, and update you on Amy's progress.
Thanks for all you do. Regards,

S.L.
july 1996

Appendices

Appendix I

Dr. Charles Armao Brusch
(1902-1993)

Dr. Charles A. Brusch, a distinguished physician from Cambridge, Massachusetts (USA), who worked with Rene Caisse for twenty years, was a pioneer in the field of cancer therapy research.

Brusch was an avid proponent of preventive medicine, with ideas that can be considered quite modern for the era he lived in. He was the first American doctor to distribute the first commercial injection of the polio vaccine in the U.S., he founded the first medical clinic for the Order of St. George in the western hemisphere, he founded the first acupuncture research centre, and owned the Brusch Medical Center in Cambridge, the largest medical clinic in the state of Massachusetts. He also was President John F. Kennedy's personal physician.

Dr. Brusch was known as a very dedicated man, who has done much to improve the lot of his fellowmen. Especially for the poor, who were unable to pay for medical care, he founded the first so-called 'prepaid medical plan' and founded a special clinic.

Brusch is a graduate of St. Lawrence University (class of 1934) with a Bachelor of Science. He obtained his medical degree from Tufts University Medical School. He specialized in surgery, internal medicine, gynecology, and psychiatry.

Amongst others, he published the following articles: The History of Chemistry (American Journal of Pharmacology, Nov. 1955); A Critical

Evaluation of Fluoridation (American Journal of Pharmacology, Nov. 1955); Combined Treatment of Gastroduodenal Ulcers (Review of Gastroenterology, 1940); and many other articles about arthritis, nutrition, and allergies.

The long list of decorations awarded to Dr. Brusch includes, amongst others: an honorary mention by the Governor's Council for thirty plus years of unexcelled medicine care to the citizens of the common wealth of Massachusetts and for professional achievement and philantropic works of exceptional caliber; the Dante Alighieri Society has recognized him for his literary, philanthropic and medical contributions; an Alumni Acknowledgment by St. Lawrence University, New York (1983) for 'outstanding achievement and service' - in the medical field. Brusch was a member of many medical organizations, including the American Medical Association.

During Brusch's 54-year career as a doctor, over a million patients were treated in his clinic. He cooperated closely with Rene Caisse from 1959 onwards. After Rene's death in 1978, Dr. Brusch continued researching the effects of the eight-herb formula in his laboratory. In 1988 he relinquished the formula and its distribution rights to Elaine Alexander, with several other herbal formulas and products that he had researched in his clinic for years.

Regarding his research of the eight-herb formula, Brusch has written the following:
'This eight-herb formula was used for the treatment of cancer and was also researched by numerous doctors who treated thousands of patients. These treatments have been documented by doctors, by individuals who have been cured, and by members of patients' families who can testify to the effects of the herb formula. Documentation included many cases, including a history of the physical examination, laboratory findings, x-rays, clinical findings and progress notes.

In 1958 Rene Caisse began working at the Brusch Medical Research Center. At the time we commenced our research project to prove the merits of the eight-herb formula in the treatment of cancer. We used the herbal medicine as an oral treatment: two ounces of the herb formula each night in one-half to one glass of warm water, with no other medication, on an empty stomach. A little later we were anxious to find out what the active ingredients were. So we experimented with injectible solutions, each vial containing a different herb in the herb solution. We failed to isolate a single outstanding herb. We found out that reactions and results were not so good so we stopped injections with the isolated herbs and returned to using the oral medication. Experimenting with the single herbal injections proved to us that best results were obtained by the combination of herbs contained in the eight-herb formula and not in one single active herb.

Good results obtained by taking the herbal medicine included cessation of pain, increased appetite, weight gain, feeling of well being which reflected improved emotional attitudes regarding depression, anxiety, and fear, and prolongation of life. Results improved with the continuance of the herb formula medication.

The herb formula research program at Brusch Medical Centre was carried on by Rene Caisse and myself, Director of Research; by Dr. Charles McClure, former professor of Gastroenterology and Research at Boston University Medical School and Peter B. Brigham Hospital, a member of Who's Who in World Medicine; by Dr. P. Pappas, former Professor of Urology at Tufts Medical School, affiliated with New England Medical Center; by Dr. George Ceresia, Ph.D., Professor of Chemistry, Albany School of Chemistry, affiliated with Union University, Schenectedy, New York.

Here at Brusch Medical Centre, animal experimentation was conducted with good results on 35 mice. We decided to have experimentation with animals checked so additional experimentation was conducted at the

Sloan-Kettering Institute of Cancer in New York and by Bioran Blood Chemistry Laboratory in Cambridge, Massachusetts.

With each patient who was a candidate for treatment with the herb formula we conducted a thorough physical examination, including blood analysis, EKG, x-rays, and any other clinical test that seemed pertinent.

Whenever a patient was referred to us we always obtained a history of past treatments and when possible, we would send to the doctor concerned a history of results obtained at Brusch Medical Center. Oftentimes, when the patient returned to his home town or state, the attending doctor would send us progress notes.

The Sloan-Kettering studies with mice were done in June, 1975. One hundred eighty mice were used in the study that showed a recession of growth of tumors.

We were satisfied with these results although we know that results obtained in animals do not always equate response in humans. In the case of animals, tumors are bred in selected species and so animal tumors are definitely different from tumors in humans. In humans we deal with many complicated issues; often other diseases such as arthritis, allergies, diabetes, nervous tension are present and affect the tumorous condition, something that was not present in selected animals.

In summary, the eight-herb tea, a non-toxic herbal formula used in the treatment of cancer is not incompatible for use with other medications, radiation, chemotherapy, x-rays, or any other known treatment. It can be used for an indefinite period of time, does not spoil, is easy to administer, is inexpensive, can be administered by a doctor or taken by prescription.

At one period of experimentation we also used a double blind study in which we used other herb formulas, all of which proved to be inferior to the herb formula. In some cases we used medication in form of tablets or placebos with no results.

I feel that the experimentation with the eight-herb formula was an outstanding piece of work considering the wonderful effects achieved by using the herb formula. For over 65 years the formula was used constantly by doctors, proving its merits of healing and non-toxic effects. Studies carried on in Canada and in the United States, two different countries, gave the same results.

In a June, 1982 radio program known as PRN, fakery in research was aired, showing that research projects on cancer, some done independently and some by medical schools, gave many false statistics in projects for which millions of dollars had been appropriated. We had no grants given to us; all studies, including those done in two different countries, in different laboratories, by different doctors, were conducted with strictly ethical procedures and everything could be re-checked.

The results we obtained with thousands of patients of various races, sexes, and ages, with all types of cancer, definitely prove the eight-herb formula to be a cure for cancer. All studies done in four laboratories in the United States and one or more in Canada fortify this claim.'

Charles A. Brusch, M.D.

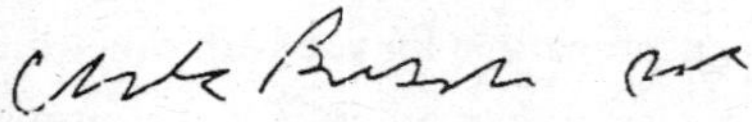

Appendix II

Elaine Alexander
(1924-1996)

When Elaine Alexander first contacted Dr. Brusch in 1984, she had been working as a broadcaster and producer for Canadian radio for twenty years. Rene Caisse's story and the exceptional herbal tea had drawn her interest and she had schooled herself well in the subject.
By then, Elaine had already had several careers: she had worked as a model, studied speech therapy and worked as a professional singer, until she started working as a radio producer for the much-discussed program Hotline, which was known for its controversial and highly informative subjects. Big names like Martin Luther King, President Harry Truman, Mohammed Ali, and Linus Pauling, have all been guests in Elaine's program.

ne Alexander and Flora- aging director mas Greither

In 1984, Elaine had just started a new informative program called Stayin' Alive, which concentrated on health items.
Established experts came to Elaine's studio and engaged in live discussion on air with listeners who phoned in. Amongst others, Elaine had Dr. Luc Montagne, the French discoverer of the AIDS virus, in her

program, but she also talked to many proponents of alternative medicine. She never avoided any subject or discussion.

Elaine cared very deeply about Rene Caisse and the herbal formula. She had studied the subject very closely and had got to know Rene well from stories told by former patients. The interview between Elaine and Dr. Brusch was the very first interview ever that Dr. Brusch had given. In this interview, Dr. Brusch openly declares: 'This herbal formula is a remedy for cancer. I wouldn't have believed it myself if I hadn't seen it with my own eyes.' The impact of this interview and the interviews that followed was enormous. Listeners even drove their cars to the studio because all telephone lines to the studio were occupied while the show was on.

Like Rene, Elaine was so dedicated that she turned her life upside down completely to start providing reliable information about the herbal formula on a fulltime basis. She worked day and night to answer phonecalls from all over the world, send tea to users by mail order, give lectures, write articles, and answer the many questions users asked her by mail or telephone.
Only those very close to her knew that that was emotionally as well as physically a very heavy task. Elaine called those hectic years when patients would literally cry on her doorstep, the hardest years of her life.
Thanks to Elaine's efforts, in cooperation with Dr. Brusch, and later with Flora Manufacturing & Distributing, the herbal formula is now available and known to the public at large. Like Rene would have wanted it: available for all, at a reasonable price.

Appendix III

Flora Manufacturing & Distributing

Flor.Essence is manufactured by Flora Manufacturing and Distributing Ltd, stationed in Burnaby, British Columbia in Canada. Flora employs 150 people, making it Canada's largest manufacturer of natural products. Flora was the first company in North America to produce cold-pressed organic oil. In addition, Flora manufactures many standardized herbal products, if possible using organic produce: phytotherapeutical products, herb teas, tonics and elixirs, dietary supplements, herb supplements, natural cosmetics, and most importantly, Flor.Essence.
Flora products are distributed in 55 countries. They are mainly sold in health food stores.

Flora Manufacturing and Distributing was founded in 1966 and is directed by Thomas Greither and his wife Lauren. Flora's roots are in Europe, where grandfather Greither devoted his life entirely to herbs and in 1916 founded a company for the manufacture of natural herbal products. Quality and purity, from cultivation through to the final product, are still the mainstays of the Greither production philosophy. Maximum quality is the starting point for success and effectiveness.
A second Flora branch was opened in 1988 in Lynden, Washington, in the USA. This is also the site of Flora's organic herb gardens, which are open to the public.

Flora is a an official manufacturer of organic products and is monitored by Quality Assurance International (QAI). This warrants that all ingredients of Flora products are guaranteed free of chemicals, from cultivation of the seeds right through to harvesting time. The production process, packaging and distribution also have to conform to strict norms. Flora maintains quality norms that are higher even than strictly required by law. Flora is GMP-recognized, which guarantees that all aspects of the production process comply with international norms for Good Manufacturing Practices (GMP).

To obtain organically cultivated herbs, Flora has agreements with organic farmers, guaranteeing maximum organic quality and continuity. In addition, Flora has its own herb gardens and plantations, such as Flora Farm in Aldergrove, British Columbia. When the organic raw produce arrives at the Flora plant, it is immediately quarentined. The quality control department takes samples and tests these for physical characteristics (e.g. color), chemical qualities (e.g. presence of pesticides or heavy metals), microbiological characteristics (e.g. bacteria and yeasts), and active ingredients. Only those herbs that meet all requirements may be used for the final product.

Production of Flor. Essence, in cooperation with Elaine Alexander, started in 1992 and was perfectly in keeping with company philosophy: delivering high quality natural products for personal health and recovery.

In God we trust

The mission of Flora Distributors is to Participate in the Continuing Evolution of the People on Earth toward Universal Harmony, Peace and Perfection by Providing Products and Services for the Purification and Upliftment of the Body and the Spirit, and by Providing to each Person who derived a Livelihood with Flora, an Opportunity for Personal Growth and Advancement of these Goals in Life.

Appendix IV

Scientific reports

A) Preclinical study Flor-Essence (Dry herbal blend)

Health Ministry of the Russian Federation Research Institute of Traditional Methods of Treatment
Laboratory of Physico-Chemical Analysis of Vegetal Materials and Drugs.

Victor P.Pakhomov M.D. Ch.D.

1. Specific Pharmacological Activity of Flor.Essence dry herbal tea blend (Flor.Essence)

1.1. Immunostimulating Activity of Flor.Essence
1.1.1. Effect of Flor.Essence on the Humoral Immunity
1.1.2. Effect of Flor.Essence on Cell Immunity
1.1.3. Effect of Flor.Essence on Functional Activity of Phagocytes *(effect on phagocytic activity of macrophages and effect on spontaneous migration and hemotaxis of neutrophils)*
1.2. Adaptogenic Properties of Flor.Essence
1.2.1. Effect of Flor.Essence on Working Capacity and Physical Endurance
1.2.2. Effect of Flor.Essence on Hypoxia Resistance
1.3. Effect of Flor.Essence on Bile Excretion in Rats
1.4. Effect of Flor.Essence on Motor-Evacuatory Function of the Gastrointestinal Tract
1.4.1. Effect of Flor.Essence on the Motor-Evacuatory Function of the Gastrointestinal Tract in Mice

1.4.2. Purgative Effect of Flor.Essence
1.5. Antitoxic Effect of Flor.Essence
1.6. Analgesic Properties of Flor.Essence
1.7. Spasmolytic Effect of Flor.Essence
1.8. Antiinflammatory Properties of Flor.Essence
1.9. Effect of Flor.Essence on the Repair Processes in Gastric Mucosa
1.10. Some Mechanisms of Antiinflammatory Action of Flor.Essence
1.10.1. Effect of Flor.Essence on Capillary Permeability
1.10.2. Antihistamine Properties of Flor.Essence
1.11. Effect of Flor.Essence on Diuresis and Electrolyte Balance

2. General Pharmacological Properties of Flor.Essence

2.1. Effect of Flor.Essence on the Central Nervous System
2.1.1. Effect of Flor.Essence on Spontaneous Motor Activity in Mice
2.1.2. Effect of Flor.Essence on the Effects Induced by a Reference Soporific Drug (Chloryl Hydrate)

3. Effect of Flor.Essence on the Cardiovascular System

1.1.1. Effect of Flor.Essence on the Humoral Immunity.

The experiments are based on the well-known model of thymus-dependent immunity, which is executed by macrophages, T and B lymphocytes. The effect of Flor.Essence on the humoral immunity was studied in three experimental series. The experiments showed that Flor.Essence injected intraperitoneally increased the number of AFC in the spleen by 27.9, 34.9 and 35.8%, respectively, the serum titer of hemagglutinins being elevated by 50.5, 93.8 and 96.9%, respectively.

Thus, the experiments demonstrated the stimulating effect of Flor.Essence on humoral activity.

1.1.2. Effect of Flor.Essence on Cell Immunity.

Two experimental models were used: delayed-type-hypersensitivity (DTH) reaction and graft-versus-host (GVH) transplantation phenomenon.

The experiments showed that intraperitoneal injections of Flor.Essence in all applied doses potentate the DTH reaction, the maximal effect being produced by the minimal dose of the preparation. The intragastric administration also stimulated the DTH reaction, but its effect was less pronounced.

The data suggest that Flor.Essence Dry Herbal Blend in all applied doses increased the index of DTH reaction, which is indicative of enhanced cell-mediated immune response. From these experimental data a conclusion can be made regarding immunostimulatory activity of Flor.Essence Dry Herbal Tea Blend in both enteral and parenteral administration. The effect of the preparation on cell immunity is more pronounced.

1.1.3. Effect of Flor.Essence on Functional Activity of Phagocytes

1.1.3.1. Effect of Flor.Essence on Phagocytic Activity of Macrophages:

The data suggest that Flor.Essence administered through either route enhanced phagocytic activity of macrophages, the phagocytic index being increased 1.75- and 1.55-fold in intraperitoneal and intragastric administration, respectively.

1.1.3.2. Effect of Flor.Essence on Spontaneous Migration and Hemotaxis of Neutrophils:

Flor.Essence enhances both spontaneous and chemotactic activity of bone marrow neutrophils, i.e. stimulates their functional activity.

1.2. Adaptogenic Properties of Flor.Essence

1.2.1. Effect of Flor.Essence on Physical Capacity and Endurance:

The data allow to conclude that Flor.Essence improves physical capacity in experimental animals.

The data attest to markedly imporved physical endurance caused by Flor.Essence pretreatment. Thus, experiments on mice showed that Flor.Essence in dose range of 5 tot 50 ml/kg improved physical capacity and endurance.

1.2.2. Effect of Flor.Essence on Hypoxia Resistence:
The data suggest that the preparation used in both doses exhibits the antihypoxic effect under conditions of hypoxia-hypercapnia.

1.3. Effect of Flor.Essence on Bile Excretion in Rats:
The experimental data suggest that the preparation administered intragastrally in doses of 6-30 ml/kg had practically no effect on bile excretion in rats. Only a slight tendency toward an increase was noted.

1.4. Effect of Flor.Essence on the Motor-Evacuatory Function of the Gastrointestinal Tract

1.4.1. Effect of Flor.Essence on the Motor-Evacuatory Function of the Gastrointestinal tract in Mice:
The experiment showed that the preparation in a dose of 5 ml/kg had practically no effect on the intestine motility, while in an dose of 25 ml/kg somewhat increased it.

1.4.2. Purgative Effect of Flor.Essence:
The preparation in doses of 6 and 30 ml/kg had no effect on the consistence of feces, while more loose feces were found 18 hours after administration of 60 ml/kg Flor-Essence Tea. This attests to a mild purgative effect of large doses of Flor.Essence.

1.5. Antitoxic Effect of Flor.Essence:
The duration of hexenal-induced sleep (used to determine the extent of the toxic liver damage) in both experimental groups was shown to be shorter than in group 2 (without Flor.Essence treatment). The hepatotoxic agent markedly prolongs the hexenal-induced sleep in controls in comparison with the intact animals, while both experimental groups only slightly and unreliably differed from intact rats.

This experimental model demonstrated that Flor.Essence exhibits pronounced antitoxic activity in the studied dose range.

1.6. Analgesic Properties of Flor.Essence:
The experiments revealed a tendency toward a decrease of the pain threshold, i.e. Flor.Essence possessed no analgesic activity.

1.7. Spasmolytic Effect of Flor.Essence:

The experiment showed that Flor.Essence liquid in all studied concentrations produced no reliable effect on the magnitude of barium chloride-induced contraction, i.e. this preparation does not possess spasmolytic myotropic properties.

1.8. Antiinflammatory Properties of Flor.Essence:

(using experimental models of arthritis and peritonitis) The experiments showed that Flor.Essence liquid suppressed the development of formalin-induced arthritis. We also detected a pronounced antiinflammatory effect of Flor.Essence liquid with respect tot modeled peritonitis: the volume of serous peritoneal exudate was decreased by 27.6% for doses of 6 ml/kg and by 54.4% for doses of 30 ml/kg.

1.9. Effect of Flor.Essence on the Repair Processes in Gastric Mucosa:

The experiments demonstrated that Flor.Essence reduces the degree of gastric ulceration. It promotes the repair processes in the gastric mucosa.

1.10. Some Mechanisms of Antiinflammatory Action of Flor.Essence

1.10.1. Effect of Flor.Essence on Capillary Permeability:

The experiments showed that the test preparation inhibits dye leakage from the vascular bed. The findings suggest that the test preparation exhibits capillary-protective properties.

1.10.2. Antihistamine Properties of Flor.Essence:

The experiments showed that Flor.Essence in the studied concentrations had no effect on contractile effect of histamine, i.e. did not show antihistamine properties.

1.11. Effect of Flor.Essence on Diuresis and Electrolyte Balance:

Flor.Essence administered intragastrally in the form of a decoction stimulates diuresis in rats. The Flor.Essence liquid stimulates excretion of sodium and potassium ions, but sodium excretion was increased to a greater extent.

Thus, Flor.Essence possesses a moderate diuretic activity and has a ameliorative effect on the K+/Na+ balance in the organism.

2. *General pharmacological properties of Flor.Essence dry herbal tea blend*

2.1. Effect of Flor.Essence on the Central Nervous System

2.1.1. Effect of Flor.Essence on Spontaneous Motor Activity in Mice:
Judging from the test for spontaneous motor activity, Flor.Essence has an activating effect on animal behavior.

2.1.2. Effect of Flor.Essence on the Effects Induced by a Reference Soporific Drug (Chloral Hydrate):
The test preparation in a dose of 5 mg/kg had no reliable effect on the parameters of the soporific effect of chloral hydrate. Being applied in a dose of 50 mg/kg the Flor.Essence shortened the latency of the sleep by 41%, but had no effect on its duration.

3. *Effect of Flor.Essence dry herbal tea blend on the cardiovascular system*

(assessed from ECG parameters and arterial pressure (AP)). The experiments revealed no reliable changes in the ECG taken 30 and 60 min after administration of the test preparation in comparison with the control animals. The data suggest that administration of Flor.Essence liquid produced no reliable effect on AP in normotensive rats.

Summary

(The testresults of Flor.Essence Liquid are printed in italic)

Pharmacological activity of Flor.Essence Dry Herbal Tea Blend is experimentally tested. The dry species proposed for the study represents a mixture of 8 dried and powdered drug plants: sheep sorrel (Rumex acetosella), slippery elm bark (Ulmus rubra), burdock root (Arctium lappa), Turkish rhubarb root (Rheum palmatum), kelp (Laminaria digitata), Red Clover (Trifolium pratense), watercress (Nasturtium officinale), and blessed thistle flowers (Carduus benedictus). The preparation was studied in the form of decoction prepared as described in the Usage Instruction and was applied in doses corresponding to single, 5-fold, and 10-fold maximal single therapeutic dose for humans. The doses were recalculated with the allowance for species-specific resistance of animals in comparison with humans using standard coefficients. The Flor.Essence liquid was administered to mice in doses of 5-25-50 ml/kg (intragastrally) and 1.5-7.5-15 ml/kg (intraperitoneally) and to rats in doses of 6 and 30 ml/kg (intragastrally).

The experiments showed that Flor.Essence Dry Herbal Tea Blend within the studied dose range possesses several pharmacological activities.

Using the model of thymus-dependent immunity we showed that the preparation administered intraperitoneally in doses 1.5-7.5-15 ml and intragastrally in doses 5, 25, and 50 ml/kg during 4 days prior to immunization markedly improves cell and humoral immune response to allogenic erythrocytes (sheep erythrocytes) in CBA mice. Indeed, the number of antibody-forming cells in the spleen was increased by 20-36% *(22-38%)*, serum titer of anti-erythrocyte antibodies by 27-96% *(28-86%)*, parameters of delayed-type hypersensitivity by 50-159% *(114-266%)*. Being applied intragastrally in doses 5 and 25 ml/kg (and 50 ml/kg), the preparation 13-47% *(4-58-59%)* enhances cell immune response in the graft-versus-host reaction reproduced in CBA mice.

The preparation in doses 1.5 (intraperitoneally) and 25 ml/kg (intragastrally) stimulates phagocyte activity in non-immunized CBA mice: index of sessile macrophage phagocytic reaction is elevated by 55-57% *(94 and 58%)* and spontaneous and chemotactic neutrophil mobility by 24-71%

(68,5-56,2%). The Flor.Essence-induced stimulation of the functional activity of macrophages and neutrophils in intact animals implies that the preparation affects the systems involved in immune response formation.
The standard tests for adaptogen properties revealed high adaptogen activity of Flor.Essence. It is found that the preparation applied intragastrally in doses 5 and 50 ml/kg for 5 days improves physical capacity and endurance in mice: the duration of forced swimming with a load constituting 5% body weight on day 1 (working capacity) was increased by 42-52% *(51-57%)* and the duration of repeated swimming on day 2 (endurance) was increased 2.33 and 2.25-fold *(2.93 and 3.2-fold)*. Being applied four times in a dose of 50 ml/kg the preparation exhibits antihypoxic activity and prolongs the lifetime in mice exposed to hypoxia-hypercapnia by 19% (*21%).*
Flor.Essence exerts a pronounced antiinflammatory activity in modeled acute inflammation. Single intragastric administration of the preparation in doses of 6 and 30 ml/kg diminishes inflammatory edema of rat paws in modeled formalin-induced arthritis by 27.6-54.5% *(34-59%)* and suppressed peritoneal exudation in experimental peritonitis induced by silver nitrate *(by 16.7-50.8%)*. Intragastric application in doses of 5 and 25 ml/kg for 3 days reduces blood capillary permeability in mouse skin by 15.9-35% *(18.3-42.5%)*. Capillary-protective effect of the Flor.Essence liquid may partially underlay its antiinflammatory activity.
Pronounced antiinflammatory activity of the preparation is combined with its considerable protective effect on gastric mucosa. A 10-day course of Flor.Essence (6 and 30 ml/kg) prevents ulceration in rat gastric mucosa induced by a caffeine-arsenious mixture *(by 15-46%).*

The preparation possesses a diuretic activity. Single intragastric application of Flor.Essence liquid in doses of 6 and 30 ml/kg increases diuresis during the first hour after water load by 12.3-45% *(6.5-51.2%)* and increases 5-hour diuresis by 20% *(6.3-21.6%).* The preparation promotes natriuresis and has practically no effect on potassium ion excretion. Five-hour natriuresis was increased by 50% *(56%).*

Flor.Essence exhibits antitoxic properties. A 3-day administration of the preparation in doses of 6 and 30 ml/kg diminished toxic liver damage induced by CCl4 in rats *(by 10-23%)* (judging from the duration of hexenal-induced sleep).

Flor.Essence has an activating effect on animal behavior (judging from its effect on spontaneous motor activity in mice).

Maximal tested concentration of the preparation shortens sleep latency but has no effect on the duration of chloral hydrate-induced sleep.

Flor.Essence liquid slightly stimulates intestinal motility in mice, and being applied in the maximal tested dose produces a slight aperient effect.

Over the entire concentration range Flor.Essence does not affect biligenesis and exhibits no spasmolytic, antihistamine, and central analgesic effects.

In all tested doses the preparation does not change electrocardiographic parameters and arterial pressure in alert rats.

No symptoms of intoxication were observed in mice after a long-term administration (3-week) of Flor.Essence decoction in doses of 5-25-50 ml/kg.

Thus, the preparation Flor.Essence Dry Herbal Tea Blend exhibits immunostimulatory, adaptogenic, antiinflammatory, gastroprotective, antitoxic, and diuretic effects. The preparation is well tolerated by experimental animals.

Head of Medical Department
VILAR Research-and-Manufacturing
Association, PhD V.K.Kolkhir

Conclusions

Flor.Essence Dry Herbal Tea Blend as well as Flor.Essence Herbal Tea Blend:

1. possesses an immunostimulatory activity, the effect on cell immunity being more pronounced.
2. enhances functional activity of macrophages and neutrophils.
3. improves physical endurance and working capacity and promotes organisms recovery after exhausting exercises.
4. improves organisms resistance to various damaging factors. It possesses antitoxic, gastroprotective, hepatoprotective, and antihypoxic activities.
5. exhibits a capillary-protective effect, inhibits the development of chemically induced acute inflammation.
6. preserves homeostasis by enhancing natriuresis without changes in potassium ion excretion.
7. stimulates animal behavior judging from parameters of spontaneous motor activity.
8. does not alter electrocardiographic parameters and arterial pressure over the studied dose range.
9. administered in doses corresponding to single, 5-, and 10-fold maximal therapeutic doses produces no symptoms of intoxification in mice.

Research & Development
Institute of Medical & Aromatic Plants
Head of Medical Department PhD Med.Vladimir K.Kolkhir

Recommendations for clinical studies of Flor.Essence (dry) herbal tea blend

The data obtained from the experimental pharmacological study of Flor.Essence (dry and liquid) suggest that this preparation may be recommended for clinical studies as immunostimulator and adaptogen to treat disorders associated with weakened immune system, cachexia, and malfunctioning of the detoxification process in the liver and kidneys. The preparation may be added in particular to the complex therapy of oncological diseases and used as a remedy to promote the patient's recovery after chemotherapy and radiation.

Moreover, because of its pronounced antiinflammatory activity and its antitoxic, hepatoprotective, and moderate diuretic activities, Flor.Essence can be recommended as an antiinflammatory preparation to treat acute gastritis and inflammation of the urinary and genital tracts.

Bibliography

Flor.Essence

Thomas, Richard: The Essiac Report; unknown cancer remedy (The Alternative Treatment Information Network ATIN, Los Angeles 1993)

Ulmer, G.A.: Flor.Essence, universele geneeskracht (Uitgeverij Librena b.v. Harderwijk)

Audiotapes:

1974, June 1: Rene Caisse

Essiac - Five decades of doubt Cancer Walters / Carson

1977, June 10: Rene Caisse

1977, Aug. 21: Keeping Hope Alive

1984, Nov. 11: Essiac Part One

1984, Nov. 11: Essiac Part Two

1993: NWFA Convention, Ressurection of RC Formula / Unified Solutions

1995: Keeping Hope Alive

1995, June 6: WCBW

1995, July: WCBW

CKNW Sterling Fox and Elaine Alexander

Herbs

Academie voor Natuurgeneeskunde, lessen fytotherapie 2e jaars.

British Herbal Pharmacopoeia 1990 volume 1.

Castleman, Michael: The Healing Herbs; the ultimate guide to the curative power of nature's medicines.

Curtis, S./Fraser, R./Kohler, I.: Natuurlijk beter (Uitgeverij Ankh-Hermes bv Deventer 1995)

Foster, S./Duke, J.A.: Eastern/Central Medicinal Plants, (Peterson Field Guide, 1990)

Gids voor geneeskrachtige planten (Readers Digest)

Gursche, Siegfried: Healing with Herbal Juices (Alive Books Vancouver 1993)
Haneveld, dr G.T./Huijsen, drs L.P.: Het groot homeopathisch gezondheidsboek (A.W. Bruna Uitgevers B.V. Utrecht 1994)
Hellemont, J. van: Fytotherapeutisch compendium (Bohn Stafleu van Lognum, 2e druk)
Indros Almere, Phytotherapeutisch Vademecum (Uniepers b.v. Abcoude 1991)
Murray,M./Pizzorno, J.: Encyclopaedia of Natural Medicine (Macdonalds & Co. Publishers Ltd, Groot-BrittanniÎ 1990)
Ody, P.:Kruidengeneesmiddelen zelf maken (Uitgeverij Tirion Baarn 1995)
Oswald, E.H.: Kruidenvademecum deel 1 (Stichting Science & Nutrition Amsterdam, 1983)
Schaaf, H.J. van der: Vademecum voor de phytotherapie (Lumen Naturae b.v. Rhenen 2e herziene druk 1985)
Schmidsberger, P.: Thieme's boek van de geneeskruiden
Thurzov, L.: Lexikon der Heilpflanzen (Lingen Verlag Köln 1976)
Walters, R.: Herbs & Plants Against Cancer (Townsend Letter for Doctors, april 1991, New York)
Wichtl, M.: Herbal Drugs and Phytopharmaceuticals (Medpharm Scientific Publishers, Norman Grainger Bisset)

Indians

Davis, C.: Volkeren toen en nu; de Indianen (Uitgeverij Elsevier, Amsterdam 1983)
Dickason, O.P.: Canada's First Nations
Kubiak, W.J.: Great Lakes Indians; a pictorial guide
Lips, Eva: Indianen van Noordamerika (Uitgeverij Ankh-Hermes bv, Deventer 1979)
McLuhan, E.: Canada's Native Peoples, volume II.
Redsky, James: Great Leader of the Ojibway: Mis-quona-queb
Wilson, Roy. I.: Indiaanse medicijnwielen (Mirananda uitgevers b.v. Den Haag 1995)

Nutrition & dietary supplements

Beijer,S./Doornink,N./Vogel,J./Wipkink, A.: Voedingsgids voor mensen met kanker (Uitgeverij De Toorts, Haarlem 1994)
Rogers, Sherry A.: Chemical Sensitivity (Keats Publishing, Inc. New Canaan, Conn. USA, 1995)
Schroeder, H.A.: The poisons around us (Keats Publishers Inc. New Canaan, Conn. USA, 1978)
Erasmus, Udo: Fats that heal, fats that kill (Alive Books, Burnaby BC Canada, 1993)
Lane, Dr. William I./Comac, Linda: Sharks don't get cancer (Avery Publishing Group Inc. New York, USA, 1992)
Passwater, Richard A.: The new supernutrition (Pocket Books, New York, 1991)
Passwater, Richard A.: Cancer prevention and nutritional therapies (Keats Publishing, Inc. New Canaan, Conn. USA, 1993)
Pasteur, J.L.: 100 Vitaminekuren voor een betere gezondheid. (Zuidnederlandse Uitgeverij N.V. Aartselaar, Belgie, 1994)
Pauling, Linus: How to live longer & feel better (Avon Books, New York, 1987)
Prasad, Dr. Kedar N.: Vitamines in Cancer Prevention and Treatment. (Healing Arts Press, Rochester Vermont, USA 1994)
Peter, F.M.: Diet, Nutrition & Cancer (False Church, Virginia. American Institute for Cancer Research, Committee on Diet, Nutrition and Cancer, Assembly of Life Sciences, National Academy of Sciences, 1982)
Veer, Dr. P.H.W.A.M. de: Wij eten ons ziek (Bigot & Van Rossum, Baarn 1991)

References

Detoxification

S. Gershon, Lancet, 24 juni 1961, 1371-1374.

J.Caldwell, W.B. Jakoby, Academic press, NY, 1983.

C.D. Klaasen, M.O. Amdur et al., The Basic Science of Poisons, 3rd ed., MacMillan Publishing Co., NY, 1986.

M.Frezza, C. DiPadova et al., New Engl J Med, 1990, 322:2, 95-99.

S.A. Rogers, Int Clin Nutr Rev, 1991, 11:3, 117-125.

I.L. Prilipko et al, Acta Physiol Pharmacol Bulg, 1983, 9:4, 14-50.

W.J. Rea: Chemical Sensitivity. Vol I, CRC Press, 1992, Boca Raton.

Slippery elm (Ulmus Fulva)

R.J. Beveridge, W.A. Szarek et al., Carbohyd.Res. 1971, 19, 107-116.

B.P. Jackson, D.W. Snowdon 1990 [T9].

Burdock root (Arctium lappa)

P.D. Bryson et al., Journal of the American Medical Association, 1978, 239, 2157.

G. Dombradi, Chemotherapy, 1970, 15, 250.

K. Morita et al., Mutation Research, 1984, 129, 1-25.

F. Oprach, T. Hartmann et al., Planta Med. 1986, 52, 513.

J.D. Phillipson, L.A. Anderson, Pharm. J. 1984, 233, 80, 111.

P. Rohdewald, G. Rücker et al., Apothekengerechte Pr¸fvorschriften, S. 827, Deutscher Apotheker Verlag, Stuttgart 1986.

J. Tsujita et al., Nutrition Reports International, 1979, 20, 635.

T. Washino, H. Iwabuchi et al., Nippon Nogeikagaku Kaishi 1985, 59, 389; C.A. 103, 52880 (1985).

T. Washino, M. Yoshikura et al., Agric.Biol.Chem. 1986, 50, 263; C.A. 104, 203839 (1986).

Y. Yamada, K. Hagiwara et al., Phytochemistry. 1975, 14, 582.

Blessed thistle (Cnicus benedictus)

G. Harnischfeger, H. Stolze, Notabene medici 1981,11, 652.

G. Harnischfeger, H. Stolze, Bewährte Pflanzendrogen in Wissenschaft und Medizin. 1983, 74-81.

G. Schneider, I. Lachner, Planta Med. 1987, 53, 247.

R. Vanhaelen-Fastre, Planta Med. 1973, 24, 165 en 1974, 25, 47-59 en 1974, 26, 375-379 en 1976, 29, 179-189.

H. Wagner, S. Bladt et al., Plant drug analysis, Springer-Verlag, Berlin, Heidelberg, New York, Tokio, 1984, p.134.

A. Ulubelen, T. Berkan, Planta Medica 1977, 31, 375-377.

E. Bloszyk, B. Geppert et al., Planta Medica 1978, 34, 79-86.

Watercress (Nasturtium officinale)

E.A. Spinks, K. Sones et al., Fette Seifen Anstrichmittel 1984, 86, 228.

A.J. MacLeod, R. Islam, J.Sci.Food Agric. 1975, 26, 1545.

Doernemann, W. Löffelhardt et al., Ca.J.Biochem. 1974, 52, 916.

Rhubarb root (Rheum palmatum)

J.J. Chirikdjian et al., Planta Medica 1983, 48, 34.

J. Dong-hai et al., Pharmacology 1980, 20, 128.

R. Engelshowe, Pharm.unserer Zeit 1985, 14, 40-49.

J.W. Fairbairn, Pharmacology 1976, 14, 48.

L. Holzschuh, B. Kopp et al., Planta Medica 1982, 46, 159-161.

B.P. Jackson, D.W. Snowdon, Atlas of microscopy of medicinal plants, culinary herbs and spices, Belhaven Press, London, 1990, p.200.

Y. Kashiwada, G.I. Nonaka et al., Phytochemistry 1988, 27, 1469.

Y. Kashiwada, G.I. Nonaka et al., Phytochemistry 1988, 27, 1473.

Y. Kashiwada, G.I. Nonaka et al., Chem.Pharm.Bull. 1989, 37, 999.

Y. Kashiwada, G.I. Nonaka et al., Phytochemistry 1990, 29, 1007.

I. Kubo, I. Soediro et al., Phytochemistry 1992, 31, 1063.

I. Kubo, Y. Murai, J.Nat. Prod. 1991, 54, 1115.

G.I. Nonaka, I. Nishioka et al., Chem.Pharm.Bull., 1981, 29, 2862.

F.H.L. van Os, Pharmacology 1976, 14 (Suppl. 1)7-17.

H. Oshio, S Imai et al., Chem.Pharm.Bull. 1974, 22, 823-831.
K. Sagara, T. Oshima et al., J.Chromatogr. 1987, 403, 253-261.
E. Stahl, H. Menflen et al., Dtsch. Apoth. Ztg. 1985, 125, 1478.
E.H.C. Verhaeren, M. Dreessen et al., Planta Medica 1982, 45, 15.
T. Yamagishi, M. Nishizawa et al., Chem. Pharm. Bull. 1987, 35, 3132-3138.

Kelp (Laminaria digitata)

J.F.Biard et al., Planta Medica 1980, Suppl:136.
P.Erbes, W. Boland, Helv. Chim. Acta, 1992, 75, 766-772.
S. Funayama, H. Hikino, Planta medica 1981, 41, 29.
N. Iritani, J. Nogi, Atherosclerosis 1972, 15, 87.
I. Maier, D.G. Müller et al., Z.Natur-forsch. 1994, 49c, 601-606.
P.B. Searl et al., Proceedings of the Western Pharmacology Society 1981, 24,63.
K. Stratmann, W. Boland et al., Angew. Chem., 1992, 104, 1261-1263.
A. Sutton et al. International Journal of Padiation Biology 1971, 19,79.

Red clover blossom (Trifolium pratense)

P. Dewick, Phytochemistry 1977, 16, 93.
J. Duke, HerbalGram 1989, 18/19, 13.
J. Hartwell, J. Lloydia 1970, 3, 97.

Astragalus (Astragalus membranaceus)

D. Chu et al. Clin. Immuno and Immunopathology 1987, 45, 48-57.
D. Chu et al. J.Clin Lab. Immunol. 1988, 25, 125-129.
D. Chu et al. Chung Hsi I Chieh Ho Tsa Chih 10, 34-36.
B. Lau et al. Phytotherapy Research 1989, 3, 148-153.
J.R. Rittenhouse, P.D. Lui et al., J Urology 1991, 146, 486-90.
Y. Sun, E. Hersh et al., Cancer July 3, 1983, 52, 70-73.
Y. Wang, X. Qian et al., Mol Biother 1992, 4, 143-46.
Z. Zhang, Q.Wen et al., J Ethnopharmacology 1990, 30, 145-49.
K.S. Zhao, C. Mancini et al., Immunopharmacology 1990, 20, 225, 34.

Echinacea (Echinacea angustifolia)

E. Samochowiez et al., Wiadmosci Parazytologizne 1979, 25(1), 77.

E. Trangni et al., Food and Chem. Toxic 1985, 23(1), 317.

A. Wacker, A. Hilbig, Planta Medica 1978, 33, 89.

H. Wagner, A. Proksch, Angew. Phytother 1981, 2(5), 166.

Ginseng (Panax ginseng)

Bensky, Gamble & Kaptchuk `Chinese Herbal Medicine' Materia Medica, Eastland Press, Seattle USA (1986) pg 452.

C.S. Cheung, Y-K Lai, Traditional Chinese Medical Publisher, San Francisco CA, USA (1980) pg 67.

S. Fulder, The Am J of Chinese Med 1981, 9, 112-118.

F.P. Smith, G.A. Stuart, 'Chinese Medicinal Herbs' Georgetown Press, San Francisco CA, USA (1973) pgs. 302 & 304.

Green tea (Camellia sinensis)

M. Amella et al, Planta Medica 1985, 51, 16-20.

H. Graham, Preventive Medicine 1992, 21, 3, 334-350.

G. Hu et al., Nutrition and Cancer 1995, 24, 203-9.

E. Middleton, G. Drzwieki, Int. Arch. Allergy Appl. Immunol. 1985, 77, 155-157.

Statistical Yearbook of Agricultural, Forestry and Fishery in Shizuoka Pref., Kanto-Noseikyoku Shizuoka-Tokei-Kyokai (1979).

Ministry of Health and Welfare, Japan Vital Statistics Serues, Kosei-Tokei-Kyokai (1969-1982).

I. Oguni et al. Abstracts of Papers, the Annual Meeting of the Agricultural Chemical Society of Japan, Sapporo, July 1985, 153; Proc.of International Tea-Quality-Human Health Symposium, Hangzhou, China November 1987, 222-226.

I. Oguni, K. Nasu et al., 'A preliminary study on the protection against cancer risk by green tea drinking.'

N. Horiba, Y. Maekawa et al., Journal of Endodontics 1991,17, No 3. March.

Cat's claw (Uncaria tomentosa)

Journal of ethnopharmacology, 1993, vol.38, 1, 63-77.

New polyhydroxylated triterpenes from Uncaria tomentosa. Journal of Natural Products, Volume 53, 3, 1990, pgs. 559-564.

R. Aquino et al., Journal of Natural Products 1981, vol.54, 2, 453-459.

P. Tampo, et al., Universidad Nacional Mayor de San Marcos, 1992.

Misteltoe (Viscum album)

T.Hajto, Oncology 1986, 43, 51-65.

T.Hajto, G. Lanzrein, Oncology 1986, 43, 93-97.

H.Hulsen, F. Mechelke, Arzneimittel-Forsch 1982, 32, 1126-1127.

T.A. Khwaja, C.B.Dias et al., Oncology 1986, 43, 42-50.

R.Lerot, Helv Chir Acta 1977, 44, 403-414.

J.Nienhaus, M.Stoll et al., Experientia 1970, 26, 523-525.

G.Ribereau-Gayon et al., Oncology 1986, 43, 35-41.

Milk thistle (Carduus marianus)

R. Campos et al., Planta Medica 1989, 55, 417.

G. Vogel, I.Temme, Arzeim.-Forsch.1969, 19, 613-615.

C. Hruby, Forum 1984, 6, 23.

F. Canini et al., Clin. Ther.1985, 114, 307.

P. Ferenci et al., J. Hepat. 1989, 9, 105.

Pau d'arco (Tabebuia avellenedae)

R.K. Morrison et al., Toxicol Appl Pharmacol 1970, 17, 1-11.

O.G. de Lima et al., Anais da Sociedade de Biologica de Pernambuco 1956, IV,129-135.

H. Gershon, L. Shanks, Can J Microbiol 1975, 21, 1317-1321.

M. Lagrota et al. Rev Microbiol 1983, 14, 21-26.

A.R. Schuerch, W. Wehrli, J Biochem 1978, 84, 107-205.

M.I.S. Linhares, C.F. De Santana, Revista Instituto Antibioticos, 1975, Refcife 15, 25-32.

A. Shapiro et al., Protozool 1982, 29, 85-90.

Shiitake, reishi, maitake

J.Smith, P. Callinan, De Orthomoleculaire Koerier 1991, 31, 14-16.

Licorice (Glycyrrhiza glabra)

J. Cyong, Intern J of Acupuncture and Electrotherapy Research 1982, 7, 173-202.

H.Hayashi, N.Hiraoka et al., Plant Sci 1996, 116, 233-238.

A. Kumagai et al., Endocrinology Japan 1976, 14, 39-42.

L. Mitscher et al., Journal of Natural Products 1980, 43, 259-269.

R. Pompeii et al., Experentia 1980, 36, 304-305.

Beta carotene

H.S. Garewal, F.L. Meyskens, Cancer Epidemiology, Biomarkers and Prevention 1992, 155, 59.

R.Harris et al., Nutrition and Cancer 1991, 15, 63-8.

T.Hirayama, Nutr. Cancer 1979, 1, 67-81.

G.S.Hughes, Nutr. Rep. 1992, 10(1), 1-8.

R.B.Shekelle et al., Lancet Nov. 1981, 2, 1185, 90.

N.J. Wald, J. Boreham et al., British Journal of Cancer 1984, 49, 321-24.

G.Wolf, Nutrition Reviews 1992, 50(9), 270-4.

Genistein

R. Bowen et al., Proc Am Assoc Cancer Res 1993, 34, 555.

A. Cassidy et al., Fed Am Soc Exp Biol 1993, 7, A866.

L. Coward et al., J Agric Food Chem. 1993, 41, 1961-1967.

T. Fotis et al., Proc Nat Acad Sci 1993, 90, 2690-2694.

M. Messina et al., Nutr.Cancer 1994, 21, 113-131.

H.K. Naik et al, Anti cancer Res 1994, 14, 2617-2620.

H. Wei et al., Nutr Cancer 1993, 20, 1-12.

Selenium

E.Burke, Nutrition Report, Oct. 1992, 10(10), 73, 80.

J.A. Milner, Journal of Agricultural and Food Chemistry, May-June 1984, 32, 436-42.
M.P. Rayman, British Medical Journal, Feb 1997, 314, 387-8.
R.L.Shamberger, C.E.Willis, CRC Crit.Rev.Clin.Lab. Sci. 1971, 2(2), 211-21.
J.T. Salonen, G. Alftan et al., American Journal of Epidemiology 1984, 120, 342-49.
W.C. Willett et al., Lancet July 1983, II, 130, 4.
S.Yu et al., Biological Trace Element Research, Jan/Feb 1985, 7, 21-9.

Vitamin C

G. Block, Am. Journal of Clinical Nutrition 1991, 53, 270S-2828S.
D.E. Henson, G. Block et al., Journal of the National Cancer Institute, April 1991, 83, 8, 547, 50.
P.M. Newbern, V. Suphakarn et al., Nutrition and Cancer 1983, 5, 107-17.
H. Padh, Nutrition Reviews March 1991, 49, 3, 65-70.
L. Pauling, E. Cameron, Proceeding of the National Academy of Sciences, 1976, 73, 10, 3685-9.
R.J. Shamberger, F.F. Baughman et al., Proceedings of National Academy of Sciences 1973, 70, 1461-63.
A.J. Verlangieri, M.J. Fay et al., Life Sciences June 1991, 48, 23, 2275-81.
R.H. Yonomoto, P.B. Chretien et al.., Proceedings of the Am. Society of Clinical Oncology, 1987, 288.

Vitamin E

A. Bendich, Nutrition Report, March 1987, 5(3), 17, 21.
P.M. Horvath, I. Clement, Cancer Research, Nov.1983, 43, 5335-41.
P. Knekt et al., Am. Journal of Epidemiology 1988, 127, 28-41.
P. Knekt, Annals of Medicine 1991, 23, 3-12.
J. Milei et al., American Heart Journal 1986, 111, 95-102.
G.M. Paganelli, G. Biasco et al., Journal of the National Cancer Institute 1992, 84, 47-51.

Choline

L. Poirier, Am. Institute of Cancer Research Newsletter , Summer 1991, 32.

A. Ghoshal, T. Rushmore et al., Cancer Letters 1987, 36, 289-96.

Folic acid

D. Heimburger et al., J.Amer. Med.Assoc. March 1988, 259, 10.

Y.I. Kim, American Journal of Clinical Nutrition Jan 1997, 65, 46-52.

Quercetine

S. Uddin, M.A. Choudhry, Biochemistry & Molecular Biology International, July 1995, 36, 545-50.

Chlorophyl

V. Breinhold et al., Cancer Research, 1995, 55, 57-62.

Nutrition

A.V. Rao, M-K. Sung, Journal of Nutrition 1995, 125, 717S-24S.

Glossary

antioxidant	A compound which prevents free radical or oxidative damage.
atherosclerosis	A process in which fatty substances like cholesterol are deposited in the walls of medium to large arteries, eventually leading to blockage of the artery.
arthritis	Inflammation of joints due to infections, metabolic or constitutional causes.
biopsy	A diagnostic test in which tissue or cells are removed from the body for examination under a microscope.
candidiasis	A complex medical syndrome produced by a chronic overgrowth of the yeast Candida albicans.
capillary	Any of the smallest blood vessels connecting arterioles with venules and forming networks throughout the body.
carcinogen	Any agent or substance capable of causing cancer.
choline	A pseudo-vitamin involved in the metabolism of fats and in nerve function, and found in lecithin.
colitis	Inflammation of the colon which is usually associated with diarrhoea with blood and mucus.
Crohn's disease	Condition characterised by an inflammatory reaction throughout the entire thickness of the bowel wall.
cross-linking	Bonds that form across molecules and result in complex molecular structures. Also, bonds that make tissue more rigid, leading to aging.

degenerative disease	Loss of the capacity of cells, tissues and organs to function normally.
diverticulosis	An intestinal disorder characterized by the presence of many abnormal pouch or sac openings.
essential fatty acids	(EFA) Fatty acids which the body cannot manufacture - linoleic and linolenic acids.
fiber	Any of several undigestible complex carbohydrates that make up the roughage of plant material and promote a.o. bowel regularity.
free radicals	Highly reactive molecules that can bind to and destroy cellular compounds.
glucose tolerance factor	(GTF) The body's ability to metabolize glucose.
glutathione	A peptide that plays an important role in biological oxidation-reduction processes and as a coenzyme.
hypoglycemia	Abnormal decrease of sugar in the blood.
insulin	A hormone secreted by the pancreas which lowers blood sugar levels.
leucocyte	White blood cell.
macrophage	A phagocytic (see phagocytose) tissue cell that may be fixed or freely motile, which is derived from a monocyte and functions in the protection of the body against infection and noxious substances.
malignant	A term used to describe a condition that tends to worsen and eventually causes death.
metastasis	A secondary metastatic growth of a malignant tumor.
Multiple Sclerosis	(MS) An auto-immune condition that leads to neural damage, motor paralysis, respiratory

	paralysis, and death.
neutrophil	A granulocyte that is the chief phagocytic white blood cell of the blood.
phagocytosis	A phagocyte is a cell (as a white blood cell) that engulfs and consumes foreign material as microorganisms and debris. Phagocytosis is the destruction of this particulate matter.
platelet	Small, colorless disks in circulating blood, which aid in blood clotting. Less sticky platelets protect against heart attacks and strokes.
premenstrual syndrome	(PMS) A nutrition-related degenerative condition affecting women before the onset of the monthly period.
psoriasis	A chronic skin disease characterized by circumscribed red patches covered with white scales.
superoxide dismutase	(SOD) An enzyme made in our body that neutralizes free radicals that could otherwise cause damage to cells.
starch	Glucose molecules hooked together into branching chains by plant cells.
T cell	A lymphocyte which is under control of the thymus gland.
trans fatty acids	Fatty acids in which the hydrogen atoms on the carbon atoms involved in a double bond are situated on opposite sides of the fatty chain.
vitamin	An essential compound necessary to act as a catalyst in normal processes of the body.

Useful addresses

For book distribution

Parole Publishing
Edisonstraat 32
3817 VN Amersfoort
tel. #31-(0)33-257 25 40
fax #31-(0)33-257 25 53
e-mail: info@parole.nl
www.parole.nl

Flora Manufacturing & Distributing Ltd.

(producer of Flor.Essence)
7400 Fraser Park Drive
Burnaby, B.C. V5J 5B9, Canada
Phone (1) 604 4366000 fax (1) 604 4366060

Acknowledgements

I am very grateful to Merel Reinink for het enthusiastic, knowledgeable and patient work on translating the book into English.
I am greatly indebted to Mr. P.J. de Jong for his dedicated critical comments while I was writing the book. In addition, I am very grateful to Pim Dekker, who was always willing to share his extensive knowledge of nutrition and dietary supplements. Petra van Marlen contributed to topics of natural medicine. I have Ellen Ankone to thank for guiding me through medical terminology.

Behind the scenes, the following people have contributed, each in their own way, to this book, and I would like to take this opportunity to thank them:
Lesley Alexander, Bas Barnasconi, Gerard Bartelds, Suzanne Diamond, Leda Fair, Thomas Greither, Floris Luiten, Paula Proulx, and Martien Witsenburg.

The author

The author holds a degree in communication studies and has been working as an editor for professional and consumer journals concerning health and nutrition since 1990 . She runs an agency for journalistic productions and public relations.